PRAISE FOR
THE HERO AND THE VILLAIN WITHIN

"Kenneth Castiel eloquently shares the benefits of making lifestyle changes for a healthy body and an extraordinary and happy life."
—DEEPAK CHOPRA, MD, AUTHOR, THE HEALING SELF

"Kenneth Castiel is a true master at growing businesses and people. In today's competitive business world, you need every advantage you can get. A great place to start is by making the most of what you have. Kenneth teaches you more workable, tangible, profitable techniques and strategies to give you the edge you need during these times of opportunity. What he teaches you about yourself and your own mindset is his true gift of wealth. He exemplifies the spirit of leadership, creativity, and enterprise."
—THE HONOURABLE FABIAN PICARDO, QC, MP,
CHIEF MINISTER OF GIBRALTAR SINCE 2011

"Kenneth Castiel is a success story with a sheer reputation for integrity. His business acumen and his ability to market built his organization in a way not previously seen in Gibraltar before. He built one of the few homegrown financial services firms in the field of investment advice that the Gibraltar finance centre had born."
—THE HONOURABLE SIR PETER RICHARD CARUANA KCMG, QC, FORMER CHIEF MINISTER OF GIBRALTAR, HOLDING OFFICE FROM 1996 TO 2011

"Kenneth Castiel is one of the most inspirational and innovative people you will ever meet. He will take you on a journey of transformation and will help you find the gem within you. Read this book and learn from one of the best."
—HESTER BANCROFT, AUTHOR, LIFE COACHING IN YOUR POCKET (FOR WOMEN), MANAGING DIRECTOR, EFFECTIVESTEPS.COM

"Kenneth Castiel is one of the most interesting people I've had the pleasure to meet. His book, The Hero And The Villain Within, is a life changer which will transform your life."
—BEDROS KEUILIAN, AUTHOR, MAN UP, FOUNDER OF FIT BODY BOOT CAMP

"Kenneth Castiel gives us a great gift: complete access to his life's work. You'll discover how to build a successful business to overcoming one of the biggest obstacles in life: self-doubt. If you are committed to winning at the game of life, Kenneth's book will be a game-changer for you."

—CRAIG BALLANTYNE, AUTHOR, THE PERFECT DAY FORMULA

"Kenneth Castiel is a business leader and a mentor par excellence. Follow him, and he will take you to even greater heights of success both personally and professionally."

—THE LATE NORMAN G. LEVINE, AUTHOR, SELLING WITH SILK GLOVES, NOT BRASS KNUCKLES, RECIPIENT OF THE JOHN NEWTON RUSSEL AWARD AND MEMBER OF THE MILLION DOLLAR ROUND TABLE

"Kenneth Castiel delivers a sage approach to freeing yourself from the chains of your villain within, and gives you the tools for you to discover your right to a life of happiness, success, and freedom. This is the book you've been waiting for. Make it your life's companion and your map to your hero within."

—MINDY HARLEY, CEO, SOCIALEMPIREONLINE.COM

"Kenneth Castiel brings deep wisdom and razor-sharp know-how to the world of business through his innovative methodology and successful track record. This is what sets him apart and makes him unique. Let him transform your life and teach you how to innovate your thinking and become the leader in your field."

—DARREN MEHLING, BA, CSCS, CEO, FREAKFITNESSONLINE.COM

"Kenneth Castiel has phenomenal discipline. He will always tell you the truth. He coached me and gave me the motivation to adopt a healthy lifestyle, while losing ten kilos and keeping it off."

—BARRY DUNLOP, MANAGING DIRECTOR, MIDASCODE LTD, LONDON, ENGLAND

"Kenneth is a businessman and a gentleman. He is one of the most tenacious and generous people I know. His staying power and sense of delivery is second to none. Stay close to him, and he will help you discover your greatness."

—ERIN NIELSON, PT, CHE, CPI, CEO, THEYOUTHMETHOD.COM

> "Kenneth Castiel taught me how to make quantum leaps in my sales productivity, while multiplying my free time."
> —PHYLLIS MILES, SENIOR FINANCIAL CONSULTANT AND MEMBER OF THE MILLION DOLLAR ROUND TABLE

> "Kenneth Castiel has got to be praised and thanked for his leadership in bringing all the warring factions together and creating the first-ever industry forum that has since spoken with one voice."
> —JOHN MILLNER, FORMER FINANCIAL SERVICES COMMISSIONER, GIBRALTAR FINANCIAL SERVICES COMMISSION

> "Kenneth Castiel walks his talk. He came to us wanting to transform his lifestyle in health and fitness and lost fifteen kilograms in just four months. He is one of the most grounded and persevering people I have ever met. He is an inspiration to work with."
> —STEPHEN EVANS, FOUNDER AND CEO, ROCK FITNESS CENTRE

THE HERO AND THE VILLAIN WITHIN

The
HERO
And The
VILLAIN
Within

YOUR KEY TO AN EXTRAORDINARY
LIFE THROUGH THE POWER OF
PURPOSE, FREEDOM AND ABUNDANCE

Kenneth Castiel

COPYRIGHT © 2018 KENNETH CASTIEL
All rights reserved.

THE HERO AND THE VILLAIN WITHIN
Your Key to an Extraordinary Life Through the Power of Purpose, Freedom and Abundance

ISBN   978-1-5445-1006-4 *Hardcover*
           978-1-5445-1004-0 *Paperback*
           978-1-5445-1005-7 *Ebook*

To my wife Maxine, my children Ben, Daniella, and Sarah, and my parents Elias and Iris

Contents

Introduction: There Is Another Way.................................... 17

PART ONE: WHERE ARE YOU NOW?............................ 29

Chapter One: Are You Ready to Wake Up?............................31
The Hypnosis of Social Conditioning

Chapter Two: How Can You Wake Up? 73
The Power of the Unconscious Mind

PART TWO: WHERE DO YOU WANT TO GO? 91

Chapter Three: Where Are the Village Elders? 93
Finding Your Higher Purpose and Creating a Far-Reaching Legacy

Chapter Four: Are You the Hero of Your Own Journey?..... 119
Your Key to Transformation

PART THREE: HOW WILL YOU GET THERE?............. 149

Chapter Five: This Could Save Your Life 151
Create Happiness through Health and Fitness

Chapter Six: What Is Your Excuse? 177
Let's Create More Time in Your Life

Chapter Seven: Abundance by Design 201
Financial Awareness and the Importance of Creating Resources

Conclusion: Let Your Light Shine Bright 233
You Are the One!

Epilogue: A New World 241
Acknowledgments.. 243
About the Author 245

Your world is only a reflection of you. Transform you and you've transformed your world.

—KENNETH CASTIEL

INTRODUCTION

There Is Another Way

*Do the thing you are afraid to do,
and the death of fear is certain.*
—RALF WALDO EMERSON

This book is about winning at life.

I made the decision to win at life at an early age and am passionate about helping you discover how to do the same, whatever your age and wherever you are in your life.

I am so passionate because I believe we are all bound together as family. We are *one* and responsible for one another.

Society tells us that there is only one way to live, succeed, grow old, get sick, and die. After a certain point, we are told change is neither prudent nor possible. But society is wrong. It is always the right time, no matter when, to make changes and create a financially sound, physically fit, and psychologically fulfilling life.

Our social conditioning, learned from well-meaning parents and teachers, has forced us to participate in a collective fiction that often leads to limitation and fear. Deepak Chopra, in his book *Ageless Body, Timeless Mind*, referred to it as "the hypnosis of social conditioning." I think of it as the biggest, though perhaps unintended, lie told since the beginning of time, one which we pass down from generation to generation.

By the time we are born, most things have been decided for us, including our name. Through our inherited values and beliefs, we make agreements with ourselves about who we are and what we are capable of doing, whether or not we are worthy, and who we think we should be.

As children, we go through a process of domestication that teaches us what to believe and how to behave in accordance with the opinions of others. We make agreements with ourselves based on our programming, which becomes part of who we think we are. We then proceed to create a life based on these agreements. Some of them will be empowering, helping us reach new heights. Others will limit our potential, our happiness, and our contribution to society. These forces then become what I like to refer to as the hero and the villain within.

Part of us wants us to win, but another part wants us to lose—the you who wants to get up at 6:00 a.m. to be successful and the you who hits the snooze button and sabotages your best intentions.

No matter how young or old we are, we *can* break through the limiting beliefs and agreements that have conditioned us to be less than who we are. We can create a life full of purpose, freedom, and abundance—a life that stands as a tall and powerful new paradigm, a legacy for generations to come.

In this book, I will guide you through a process of transformation that places you in the centre of your life. We will focus on maximising your health and strength, honouring yourself at every level, and identifying your purpose for the next stage of your life. Through introspection and reflection, you will realise that everything is in a state of becoming, including yourself, and will begin to move in harmony with the natural flow of the universe. Going against the flow and living a life that is untrue leads to fear, anxiety, unhappiness, illness, depression, and unhealthy behaviours.

You will learn to live your dream, like I did, and not someone else's dream, and to be the person you were born to be rather than the person you think you should be. When you leave behind the illusion of your insignificance, you embark on the hero's journey, which lies at the heart of this book. You engage with life on an upward spiral of experience and wisdom. I have included tools that will help you slay your dragon, find the treasure that lays at the centre of your life, and replace the negative agreements that may have shaped your life with a positive sense of possibility.

A fit mind and body are two sides of the same coin. We need a healthy mind to find the motivation to take care of ourselves and continue to grow, and we need a healthy body to do the things we want to do. When we are fulfilled and happy, our mind is active, and it facilitates our growth.

WHEN DO YOU THINK YOU WILL DIE?

In my workshops, I like to ask participants, "When do you think you will die? Do you think you will live until the age of seventy-nine, eighty-nine, or one hundred and nine?"

Where do you think that number came from?

When I first worked in the insurance industry, I learned that actuaries, who analyze the financial consequences of risk and uncertain events in the future, use statistical tables based on the average mortality experience of a population over a period of time to determine the age at which most men and women can be expected to die. Is that the age you unconsciously chose to leave the planet? Are you perhaps choosing to die based on an average life expectancy calculation?

I remember, many years ago, there used to be a television programme named *The Prisoner* where the captives were identified by a number and not by a name. The protagonist used to shout out to his captors, "I am not a number. I am a human being!"

Jokingly, I used to say to my actuarial colleagues, "I am not an average of life expectancy. I am a human being. I make my own lifestyle choices." They all laughed and probably thought that it was a good thing there weren't too many people like me. It would mess up their cosy system.

Perhaps other factors influenced you. When did your grandparents die? Do you have a favourite aunt who died young?

Recently, I met a friend in town with whom I had gone to school, and he commiserated with me, saying that "we only have a few good years left." I teased him and said to leave me out of his invented equation. I then jokingly made the sign of the cross in front of his face to keep his negativity away, like in a Dracula movie, and added that

I was going to carry a garlic necklace with me to put on every time I saw him coming. We had a good laugh, but I made sure he got the message.

I am adamant that I never want to be included in anyone's socially conditioned attitudes. I much prefer to take responsibility for my life and my results. I would rather be asked how I was doing with living, fun, and creativity than asked my potential life expectancy. This is a complete unknown quantity dependent on many factors, which include but are not limited to the genes I have inherited, my lifestyle, and my mindset.

An old friend of my father's, who is now in his eighties, has been saying for at least the past fifteen years that he's preparing to die. He quotes the Bible and speaks about three score years and ten, thinking it applies to him. I think he's been living in God's waiting room, looking at his watch as if he were at the dentist's clinic waiting for the receptionist to tell him it's his turn. He might as well have died already!

I'm convinced, therefore, that—to a large extent—the way we age is up to us. Whenever we start living with a number in our head telling us when we're going to die, we put limitations on our lives and create a self-fulfilling prophesy. No one deserves that. It's like putting the skids on the many wonderful things that could still happen and be achieved.

I am excited about the projects in my life that have thirty-year timelines, while most of my contemporaries are retiring and starting to shut down their lives. They put on weight, take medication, don't exercise, and believe it's what they're supposed to be doing at their age.

WHY WE DON'T CHANGE

Many people read books about making changes, but nothing happens. Why is that?

Do you engage with life as if you had a cast iron guarantee that you could not fail? One obvious reason many of us don't is the fear of failure, and it's that fear that holds us back. We're not taught how to deal with the fear we invent in our minds or how to reframe our perception of that fear. None of us want to fail; however, it's the fear of success, I believe, that is more difficult to comprehend.

I once had an employee who wasn't doing well in his sales job. When I spoke to him about it, he had no idea why he was performing poorly. Objectively, he had a lot going for him. Eventually, he took the plunge and turned things around. Six months later, he came to me and confessed that he now realised why he hadn't been successful—unconsciously, he knew how much work that success would create for him, and he didn't want any part of it. He unconsciously sabotaged his success in order to avoid long hours and working hard, even though he knew it would bring him financial rewards and a better life for him and his family.

The fear of success often undermines our best intentions as much as past failures do, stopping us from getting involved in new projects. It's important to remember that the past doesn't equal the future. Failing once doesn't mean we will fail again. Success is a numbers game. A baby learning to walk doesn't stop trying just because she fell a few times.

What we call failure is really only feedback. We can learn from feedback, grow from an experience and acquire new tools for our toolbox of life's learnings. Rather than let the illusion of failure hold us back, we must take massive action and say to ourselves, "Nothing between heaven and earth will stop me from succeeding, no matter how many times I have failed."

Another reason many of us don't change is because we make agreements with ourselves that are not empowering. We are influenced by negative programming, whether we are conscious of it or not. Self-doubt sets in, and we begin to believe we are incapable of success. We don't hold ourselves accountable to the same degree we do when we make agreements with friends or business associates. We will go to the gym to work out if we go with a friend, but if it's only for our own benefit, we don't go.

One of the biggest impediments to change is the lack of self-love. Many of us were not taught to love ourselves, or we learned that it's narcissistic to do so. We learned that it's okay to care for others, but not ourselves. As a result, we treat ourselves harshly, often without realising what we are doing. We don't nourish ourselves, we stop looking after our body, and we don't take care of our mind. We risk undermining who we truly are.

THE KEY TO TRANSFORMATION

The key to transformation is having a purpose, a big "why." Without a higher purpose in life, we become bored, depressed, anxious, and unhealthy. The moment we find purpose, everything changes for the positive.

What we do in the world—our work or job—is not who we are. We are greater than our daily tasks, activities and circumstances, whether we own a business, care for our family, or are retired, which makes finding our purpose so important. Purpose creates direction and momentum in life.

It is never too late to find renewed meaning and add value to our lives. My purpose has always been to create and become more than I currently am. It's always been important to me to take on new challenges, which is why I recently decided to go back to university at the age of fifty-nine, and I graduated with a master's degree in creative leadership at Regents University London, through their School of Psychotherapy and Psychology.

As I will make clear in this book, the way to change our universe is from within ourselves.

WHAT TO EXPECT

This book provides a holistic approach to finding freedom from within. It will help you unlock your potential and reach new heights.

The book is structured into three parts:

- Where Are You Now?
- Where Do You Want to Go?
- How Will You Get There?

In each section, you will find intuitive tools, practices, and exercises that will help you transform your thinking and free yourself of the shackles that have held you back.

As you replace the thoughts that have been holding you back with empowering agreements, you will discover and embrace a life of happiness, fulfilment, and freedom. You can choose to live a big and wonderful life and discover the person you were born to be. Indeed, buying this book is proof that your unconscious mind is ready for change!

PART ONE

WHERE ARE YOU NOW?

CHAPTER ONE

Are You Ready to Wake Up?

THE HYPNOSIS OF SOCIAL CONDITIONING

The way you think, the way you behave, the way you eat, can influence your life by thirty to fifty years.
—DEEPAK CHOPRA

Every week a young girl named Janet enjoyed having Sunday dinner with her family. She liked watching her mother prepare the roast, cutting off both ends before putting it in the oven. As Janet got older, she was curious why her mother always cut off two perfectly good portions of meat and put them back in the fridge. Why did her mother always make the roast smaller? Eventually Janet asked her mother, and she replied that she had no idea why she cut the ends off. She simply did what she had learned from her mother.

When the family gathered at Christmas, Janet decided to talk with her grandmother about how to prepare a roast. In particular, she wanted to know why her grandmother had taught her mother to cut off the ends.

"I didn't teach your mother anything," Janet's grandmother explained. "She does it that way because that is what she saw me do. When your mother was growing up, we didn't have much money and our oven was small, so small that a full-sized roast wouldn't fit inside it, so I cut off the ends of the roast in order to be able to shut the oven door. That is why your mother thought that it was the right way to prepare a roast."

Janet learned an important lesson that day, but the lesson wasn't about preparing a roast. Janet learned that it is important to question the things we do and find out where our habits and biases come from. She saw how easy it is to become programmed by invented truths.

In my family, our unhealthy habit was to end every dinner with a sweet. We never ate an evening meal without having a dessert, never thinking that it may not be good for our health. We did it that way because that is what our grandparents did. Our invented perception of what a meal should be became the reality we lived every evening.

It is important to understand the difference between a universal truth and an invented notion or belief. A belief, such as having to finish dinner with a desert, may be held by an individual or a group of people, but not necessarily by others, whereas a universal truth applies to everybody. An example of a universal truth is gravity. If two people fall off a thirty-story building, it doesn't really matter whether one is a charitable person and the other one isn't. They will both face the same tragic fate.

HABITS THAT SERVE US

When a belief becomes our truth, it can serve our life well if it is empowering. It can also create habits that hold us back or undermine our intention if it is disempowering or unwholesome. For that reason, we need to take a closer look at our inherited truths.

My father has been both my hero and my inspiration for change. Since the age of forty, he suffered from high blood pressure and diabetes. I never saw him exercise or take care of his health unless my mother made sure he ate the right thing. The problem is, could the next generation follow his lead without realising?

How many of us do that? We give up responsibility for our health and depend on medication or someone else to look after us. It is as if we don't love and honour ourselves enough to want to live a long and healthy life.

In his old age, my father's muscles wasted away, and over time he could barely get out of a chair on his own. He was in and out of the hospital for years. I knew perhaps there wasn't much that could be done about his illnesses, but I believe he could have exercised at any stage in his life and prevented his body from shutting down prematurely.

My father's lack of fitness had a powerful impact on me, and I decided that I wanted something different for my life. I knew that a sedentary lifestyle would do the same thing to me as it did to my father and would become my legacy to my children and grandchildren, who, in turn, would probably repeat the cycle. So, I educated myself about food, changed the way I ate, and kicked my sugar habit. I hired a personal trainer and worked out.

My father always told me to look after my health, but it was only after seeing him sick and suffering that I found the purpose to look after myself, honour my life, and love myself enough to taking massive action.

If you bought a new car today, would you go to the petrol station and fill it with the right fuel for the car? Would you take it to a mechanic to be serviced? We want our cars to have a long life and not break down, but why don't we do the same for ourselves?

In less than five months, I lost thirty pounds in weight, reduced my waistline from thirty-seven inches to thirty-two inches, built up muscle tone, stopped snoring, and quit taking medication for high blood pressure and cholesterol. The painful lumbar back problems I'd been suffering from for over twenty years disappeared.

I realised I had a choice in the situation and took responsibility for my well-being. I made a commitment to get healthy. I did it as much for my children as for myself. I wanted to set a different example. My great grandfather, my grandfather, and my father had all either died early or accepted illness in their lives from a young age. I wanted to establish a new legacy for the next generation, a new way of thinking in order to change the programming. To achieve this, I had to take full responsibility; the buck had to stop with me.

OUR BELIEF SYSTEMS HOLD US BACK

Our perceptions, habits, and programming often prevent us from becoming the person we were meant to be. The negative effects of inherited beliefs can limit our opportunities and reinforce fearful attitudes. Ideas surrounding retirement are a case in point.

The origin of retirement goes back to the seventeenth century. Otto von Bismarck, the German Kaiser at the time, under pressure from his socialist opponents to provide some form of financial support for older members of society, created a government-run pension system for workers who reached the age of sixty-five. It was an arbitrary age based on life expectancy at the time. Not many workers, however, lived that long, so it wasn't a big economic risk for the Kaiser. However, sixty-five has remained the age at which people are expected to stop working.

Though contemporary circumstances and life expectancies have changed considerably since the seventeenth century, in most western countries today, people retire when they turn sixty-five. The concept of retirement remains a powerful influencer on our expectations. Many of us believe that's when it's time to slow down, stop working, and start taking medication. Slowly and perhaps without realising it, we prepare to die.

Another pervasive form of programming that impacts our lives comes from the world of advertising. Advertisers think of people in terms of human capital and appeal to our fears and insecurities in order to sell us products. We are told that something is missing from our lives if we don't purchase the latest smartphone, fragrance, or a new car. We compare ourselves to the fake and manipulated perfection we see in advertisements and believe that we are not good enough if we are not equally perfect. We are influenced to either make a purchase or be unhappy.

Over time, programming becomes internalised. We become so conditioned by the influences in our lives that we judge ourselves and become the victim of our own judgement. Without realising it, we tell ourselves the same messages we've heard from our parents, our teachers, and society. We may believe that we're not worthy and can't achieve the things we want. Some of us find ourselves in abusive relationships because, on some level, we might think we deserve it. Whenever we say, "I could never do that" or "I won't succeed" or "I shouldn't apply for that job because I won't get it," it is a result of a negative, invented belief system that we have internalised. Negative programming is a huge impediment to fully becoming who we truly are.

My father had a friend who was diagnosed with a critical illness and was told that he had three months to live. He went home, put on his pyjamas, went to bed, and waited for death. He died exactly three months later to the day, without a fight. He had internalised the authoritative voice of his doctor. That's an example of how powerful programming can be. It was not what the doctor said to my father's friend that was so harmful. Rather, it was my father's friend's belief in the prognosis that probably led to the timing of his death.

I have a friend who was given a similar prognosis, but he sought a second opinion, changed his lifestyle, and fought for his life. He and his wife had fun, laughed, loved, went on vacations, and had an absolute blast. This friend lived another three years instead of the three months the doctor had predicted.

Like a frog that doesn't jump out of slowly heating water before it's too late, social conditioning happens over time, starting from the moment we are born, without our being aware of it. We simply accept the facts of our conditioning. I decided not to accept my programming, which is why I'm so passionate about helping others do the same. Life is too wonderful and important to be determined by what others tell us or by an arbitrary age the Kaiser chose over a century ago.

Not long ago, I met a good friend who works in sales. He said that he hadn't been doing well recently, but he was happy to announce that his seven years of lean times had come to an end. He had checked his calendar, and on the exact day seven years had come to an end, his sales went up.

I was less enthusiastic.

"My dear friend," I replied, "don't allow yourself to let that old spell—the cycle of seven years of lean followed by seven years of abundance—live in your mind. If you do, seven years from now, you will go down the spiral again. You will believe that because you had seven years of good times, you're due for seven years of hard times.

"Don't allow that seed to grow into a tree and dictate when you will be successful and when you won't. It is only an idea."

One has to protect oneself from archetypal stories, which can determine our life trajectory if we allow it. Like nuclear power, which can be used for good or bad, our ideas can either undermine our best intentions and programme us for failure or lift us up and empower us for success and happiness.

We must stand guard at the gates of our mind and never let anything hold us back. We should wake up every day like a lion and be the hero of our lives.

SMALL DAILY ACTIONS HAVE LONG-TERM CONSEQUENCES

Whenever we pay for fuel at a petrol station or check out at the supermarket, we are surrounded by temptation. Chocolates, sweets, crisps, and fizzy drinks fill the aisles and fight for our attention. Fresh vegetables or a small bag of carrots for the car ride are nowhere to be found. No wonder the world has seen an explosion in obesity and diabetes! We are constantly bombarded and encouraged to consume unhealthy foods, many of which carry addictive additives. Our children get hooked on sugar from a young age, assuring that corporations will make large profits and that our health care systems will be bankrupt for generations to come.

Photographs of celebrities and models influence our ideas about what our appearance should be. Unfortunately, many people, especially young people, don't realise that those photos are digitally altered to make everyone look perfect. In reality, people on the billboards are imperfect humans, just like us, but we have become conditioned to believe that they represent the look of success, happiness, and beauty in our society. We live in a celebrity culture that sets the fictional bar so high that it keeps us looking up at the pedestal. If we don't have a similar body or the right clothes, the villain within believes that there's something wrong with us and judges the victim within us harshly. As a result, we create a victim belief system that says we are inadequate or not worthy, which, of course, is far from the truth—we are all whole and complete because that is the way we were created.

Reading newspapers or watching the twenty-four-hour news channels on television is another form of programming. We rely on an editor in a distant office to choose which stories are worthy of our attention. One newspaper is like the next. Many wonderful things take place in the world every day, but no one reports on them because it is more profitable to report on bad news than good news. We all read more or less the same information, and we have the same perceptions about what is happening in our cities, states, and countries. We all worry about the same things.

Whenever I am travelling on the London underground, I see whole rows of people reading the same free newspaper. I imagine an invisible tube connecting the so-called news items to each person's brain as the information is sucked up, in order to influence that person's perception of life that day.

The news channels want to make a profit and sell advertising. The stories they choose grab our attention as a conduit for that income. If, for example, the channels didn't give terrorists exposure by repeating a story of an attack for days on end, terrorists would be starved of the attention they seek. But the channels want us hooked on advertising because they are accountable to shareholders' profits.

We let others dictate how we think, regardless of whether it makes us happy or not. The programming we're subjected to on a daily basis impacts our mental and physical health and the quality of our lives. It's time we observe ourselves and pay attention to our own lives. We need to ask ourselves where the influences in our lives come from. Who taught us how to see the world, what to eat, and what will make us happy? What is the source of our beliefs, and are those beliefs empowering? We need to become critical thinkers in order to make good choices.

Once my mother-in-law and I were having a meal together in a restaurant. She wasn't feeling well, had little appetite, and was struggling to eat the food on her plate. I told her that she should leave it, but she refused, saying her mother had taught her that it was wrong to leave food on her plate. I encouraged my mother-in-law to observe the situation. She had paid for the food, and if she didn't feel like finishing her meal, it was perfectly fine.

We should all observe our daily actions and catch ourselves being judgmental, especially with ourselves.

CHOOSING DIFFERENTLY

Over thirty years ago, my mother was diagnosed with a painful disease in her thigh bone. The doctor told her that she would live with it for the remainder of her life because there was no cure. Only a few months ago, after many years had passed, my mother decided to investigate whether a cure had been found. Because the doctor had planted a seed in her fertile mind that she would have to live with the ailment and the symptoms her entire life, she passively accepted his words. Had she not accepted his prognosis and sought a second opinion, the quality of her life may have turned out differently as even though there is still no cure, there is treatment to relieve the symptoms, which she was not aware of.

We are, in no small measure, the creators of our reality. Though it goes without saying that whenever we have a medical condition, we must treat it and listen to the advice of experts, we can also take responsibility for exploring other options, adopting a healthy lifestyle, and making choices about the reality we want to experience.

WE CAN CHANGE OUR AGREEMENTS

The agreements we make with ourselves determine the quality and direction of our lives. Some agreements are positive, some negative. We don't need to be concerned with the agreements that serve us well, are empowering, make us happy, and give purpose to our life. The agreements that hold us back and contribute to a negative belief system are the ones that deserve our attention because they need to be changed. We must become aware of the negative energy that can potentially come from programming, so we can defeat it by consciously replacing those agreements.

When we judge ourselves for not measuring up or perhaps

say to ourselves that we can't do something because we're a coward, we are the victim of a negative agreement. We have to ask ourselves where those negative ideas came from. When did we make the agreement that we were a coward? Who told us? Was it an authority figure in our life, a parent, or teacher when we were growing up? If we keep repeating to ourselves that we are a coward, how will we ever be able to attempt something new and exciting? How can we enjoy the adventure of life and grow from the challenges life presents us if we don't embrace the bold and positive energy of the hero within?

Getting offended easily, taking things personally, and attempting to read another person's mind leads to creating negative agreements with ourselves that ultimately undermine us in more ways than we can imagine. Those behaviours keep our negative agreements firmly in place. The good news is, we can exorcise the negative beliefs that hold us back and create new, empowering agreements to replace them by changing our behaviour.

THE VILLAIN VERSUS THE HERO

Don Miguel Ruiz in his book *The Four Agreements* says we should be impeccable with our word.

Imagine yourself sitting in the front row centre court at the Wimbledon tennis championships. Two players are playing for match point to win the trophy. The atmosphere is electric. All you hear is the tennis ball hitting the players' rackets at high speed as they return the volley. Your eyes are fixed on the small ball, and you can almost predict whether the player is going to hit and return it successfully another time.

Now imagine you concentrate like that every time you open your mouth to speak. Imagine events taking place in slow motion. Before words leave your mouth, in your mind's eye project the impact of the words you are about to say. What effect will they have on another person emotionally, psychologically, and physically?

What long-term effect will your words have on the person and on your relationship with the person? Will the words mark the person forever? If you are speaking with a child, will what you say influence her personality and who she becomes later in life?

If what you say has an impact on another person, imagine how the person's life might change as a result of what you say. See how the person will speak to others, including her children, as a result of what she heard from you.

Be impeccable with your language because everything we say creates either toxicity or sweetness. We can build or destroy with our words. The effect of what we say is far-reaching and can create an unintended legacy in the world for those we love and care for.

You can also programme yourself through your words, even if you are not aware that you are doing so. Deepak Chopra says that, "Every cell is eavesdropping on your internal dialogue."

It is majestic and frightening at the same time that we have such power within ourselves. Can you imagine the impact you have on your health, both physically and psychologically, every time you speak to yourself positively or negatively?

I entitled this book *The Hero and the Villain Within* because everything we say, do, or think with ourselves or others comes from negative or positive energy.

Negative energy, or the villain, wants to destroy your life without you realising it. It doesn't want you to find out how powerful you are. It wants to keep reminding you—through the programming and conditioning you've received since you were born—that you are unworthy of having the best.

Positive energy, or the hero, wants to motivate you to go for gold at every stage of your life. It comes from your unlimited potential and the fact that you are imbued with divinity. We are royalty and can do or have anything we set our minds to.

The villain and the hero are two opposing forces playing for the championship of our lives, and they are prepared to go to any length to win—one with evil intent and the other with love.

Imagine the impact of the villain on the person who smokes, takes drugs, overeats, consumes too much alcohol, or doesn't get up early in the morning. What is the villain's underlying message to that person? *You are unlovable and not worthy of anything good, so eat all the wrong foods, become obese and unhealthy, and don't take care of yourself. Look after your dog but not yourself.*

Now imagine the impact of the hero on the person who gets up like a lion at six in the morning to succeed, goes to the gym or for a run to stay fit and strong because he wants to live a long and healthy life, and looks for the good in everything and everyone. As Miguel Ruiz points out, we should never take anything personally or make assumptions, and we should always attempt to do our best.

Do you see the forces at play? One wants to kill you and the other wants you to receive your wonderful inheritance of abundance, happiness, and blessings, so that you become a blessing for everyone who comes in contact with you.

Observe yourself as you go about your life. Observe the unconscious programming that has guided your life. Put yourself in the centre court of your mind and watch how you craft your life.

Reach out to the hero within and embrace it. Make powerful choices and commitments and implement them quickly, before the villain has a chance to stop you. Become gutsy and tenacious.

Don't despair if the villain sometimes gets the better of you because it's sure to happen. Get up, brush yourself off, and fight another day. Every time we fail, the villain wants us to remain in that disempowered state. That's how it wins and proves its point to us. Use every trick in the book against the villain. The villain may seem powerful, but it isn't in reality. The villain is sly and will try and catch you out, but if you're awake and observe the game of life as a spectator, you can patiently plan and strategise. You will win and build a wise and fulfilling life with renewed purpose.

BE PRESENT

If you are not in the present moment, where are you?

> Once I was sitting in a restaurant in Jerusalem having a meal alone. A lot was going on in my life at the time, and I was deep in thought.
>
> Unexpectedly, one of the two women sitting at the table adjacent to mine turned toward me and asked me if I was speaking to her.
>
> No, I replied, but suddenly I realised that I had been gesticulating, moving my lips, and having a full-on conversation with myself.
>
> Looking back on that incident, I realised that the thoughts I was having were generating negative emotions in me which had taken over. I had gotten lost in my head and was talking to myself!
>
> I had allowed my mind to jump from one thought to another, like a monkey leaping from branch to branch. I had not been in the present moment and was completely unaware of what was going on around me.

Imagine yourself sitting in the movie theatre of your mind. You are watching a movie that you create and that exists in your mind only. You are the producer, the cameraman or camerawoman, and the audience all rolled into one, and the movie is plugged into your emotions of love, happiness, faith, compassion, anger, fear, hate, and sadness. Emotions generate energy, and that energy will inhabit our lives.

When the movie in our mind relates to the past or the future, it may not serve us well and may not be empowering and wholesome. They have little to do with what is going on in the present moment. We may feel resentful about something that happened last week—a comment from our boss or a person who offended us—and we play that movie over and over again in our mind. We do the same thing when it comes to the future; we anticipate future events and watch them unfold again and again in our mind.

In other words, we project our emotions onto the screen of our mind, and believe the movie we have created of the future to be true. If the movie is particularly intense, we could suffer from shortness of breath or a racing heart as our emotions manifest in our physical body. But the movie isn't true. Why? Because the future hasn't happened yet and is only a figment of our imagination. The movie is not reality and takes place only in our mind.

PERCEPTION BECOMES REALITY

We sometimes say that we are worried sick about something. Instead of allowing that emotion or fear to take over, become aware of your breath as you inhale and exhale. If you are walking, become aware of the steps you are taking as each foot presses down on the ground. Both your breath and your steps are happening in the present moment. Become mindful of the here and now and take refuge there.

Let me give you an example. Imagine you were sitting in

your living room watching a horror movie at one o'clock in the morning with all the lights turned off and you're suddenly thirsty. You decide to go to the kitchen for a glass of water. The corridor is dark, and you hear the sounds on the television. Chills go up and down your spine as you walk towards the kitchen, and you look behind to see if anyone is following you.

In reality, you know there is no one there. You are believing in the power of suggestion, even though you know it's not true. You're afraid because of the television programme you've been watching, not because your home is scary. The fear comes only from your mind. It's a figment of your imagination, which is what gives us a thrill when we go to Disneyworld and are happy to pay for the experience. Too often, however, we live in fear because of our imagination. Our imagination is a wonderful thing, but like with nuclear power it can either be used positively or negatively.

We humans are very suggestible. We tell ourselves that we're only watching a movie or that the fear is in our mind, but we end up believing what we see, and experience the emotions that arise. We cease to live in the present moment. We're there physically, but our mind is elsewhere. We become anxious, which is not good for our health, and we've made ourselves unhappy. Our creativity declines. The movie in our mind creates havoc. The antidote: come back to the present moment, through your breath and your steps, and allow your body and your mind to heal.

You experience the present moment through your five senses. When you close your eyes and listen to the sounds around you, the sounds are in the present moment and so are you. The sounds you hear are not in your head. You haven't invented them. Allow them to bring you back to the present moment.

Look at an object, such as a vase or a chair. The vase or chair occupies space in the here and now. Now, locate your body; your body is in the here and now. You are no longer living in the fiction created by your mind. You are free, knowing all is well.

Any concern for the future is only a thought. It's not true because it hasn't happened yet. If you're still not convinced, ask yourself where that worry will be 150 years from now.

As you drink a glass of water, feel the water on your lips and the pleasure of the liquid filling up your mouth and flowing down your throat. Be mindful of these sensations as they happen. Experience the joy of becoming aware of your wonderful body and the way it works.

Normally, all is fine in the present moment. It's only when you allow your mind to take over, wreak havoc, and invent a fiction that there's a problem. So, relax, be present, and be well!

In the big picture of life, you're always in the right place at the right time doing the right thing and receiving loving feedback from life. Sometimes the feedback can be tough, but it relates to where you are now. It's like going through school and learning at every stage.

You are a wonderful, beautiful person who deserves only good going forward. Create it because, to a very large extent, you are the creator of your universe.

TECHNIQUES FOR STAYING PRESENT

When walking down the street, be in each step you take. Feel the pressure of the ground pushing against the soles of your feet. Be conscious of every step you take as you proceed down the street. Then, you are in the present moment because the step is happening *now*. Feel the back of the chair you are sitting in as you read this book. Smell the fragrance of a flower or the cinnamon you sprinkled on your food. When you do, what you experience through your senses is happening in the here and now.

Being in the present moment is a simple thing to do. It

requires practice and patience. Don't be critical of the effort you make. Learning to be present is a process that is worth the time to master. It's where your happiness, peace, healing, and freedom are.

The present moment is an empowering and wholesome place. Our life exists in the present moment, not in the movies we create in our mind. The only true thing is where you are now. If nothing terrible is happening, why create it in your mind? Even if you live to be 150 years old, but you've been living in your mind, you won't have lived at all because you were never here. You didn't smell the roses, and you never heard the laughs. You were always in your mind, worrying and frightened, and never claimed your inheritance of peace and happiness.

A useful tool for understanding how the mind works is thinking of a surfer riding the waves.

If you were on a surfboard riding the waves, you wouldn't be able to be on another surfboard at the same time. Imagine the surfboard is your presence in the here and now. In the same way, as you can only ride one surfboard at a time, you can only be present in one place at any given moment—the present moment.

The condition of the sea you are surfing on—whether it is rough or calm—represents the life circumstances going on around you. If the sea is choppy, you have to negotiate the waves and take care that the chaotic sea doesn't distract you and knock you off your board. Similarly, events can be distracting. If you lose yourself in the chaos of your thoughts, you have fallen off the board, temporarily lost your paradise, and are no longer in the here and now.

If you focus your attention on staying on the surfboard—dealing with all of life's situations through the here and now, your place of safety and refuge—the rough sea and distracting circumstances won't affect you. You will be able to ride the waves of life. If you fall off the board, come back to the present through your breath as you inhale and exhale, through the sounds you hear, the things you see, or the sensations you feel, all of which are in the here and now.

Your ability to surf, whether it's on the ocean or on the sea of life, depends on how present you are. The state of our mind, as every Olympic athlete knows, influences our chance of victory. No surfer wants to fall off his board and miss the big wave, and we don't want to get lost in confusion and miss out on life.

When we fall off the board, all we have to do to get back on is regain our composure by coming back to the present moment.

LIVE WITH PURPOSE

Living with purpose helps bring balance to our lives. It

enables us to do the things we want to do whilst taking care of the things we must do. Purpose brings joy to life, a sense of well-being and fulfilment. It allows us to live with enthusiasm. Even though we must earn our living and manage daily chores, we can also be happy.

I love the story of President John F. Kennedy visiting the NASA Space Center. He saw a janitor carrying a broom and walked over to him. The President asked the janitor what he did there, and the janitor replied by saying that he was helping put a man on the moon.

Each of us can have a mission in life—our own unique way of changing the world to leave a lasting legacy—even if only in a small way. I agree with Napoleon Hill, author of Think and Grow Rich, who said that if you cannot do great things, do small things in a great way.

When you work hard to change, it's important to honour your successes. Just as you recognize a kindness you received from a friend and offer your appreciation, you should do the same for yourself.

Take time to celebrate your victories. You don't have to put celebration off for another day. You can go to a good restaurant or cook yourself a special meal to acknowledge a job well done. By celebrating, you pat yourself on the back, recognize your efforts and achievements, and tell yourself that you are worthy of everything good. Do so often.

Constantly give yourself positive feedback and acknowledgment just as you would for someone you love and care about. Treat yourself kindly. Feel all the love that has ever been sent to you.

BE A NONCONFORMIST REVOLUTIONARY™

You become a nonconformist revolutionary™ when you begin to change your behaviour and start to be true to who you are. You become who you were born to be, not what another person or society expects you to be.

A nonconformist revolutionary realises that we have only one life to live, and that we can make choices about how we want to live it. We either go against our desires and undermine our values because we want to fit in, or we do the things we want in life. We live with purpose and express ourselves as we wish. We all have the right to be who we want to be, to work towards creating the life that suits us, and to not be intimidated by others in any way.

I use the word revolutionary in a positive sense to refer to breaking through conventional ways of thinking. A revolutionary doesn't find it necessary to conform to the way things have always been done and isn't afraid to change, even if it may be uncomfortable. A nonconformist revolutionary is willing to make difficult choices in order to live a life of freedom and integrity.

LEVERAGE YOUR MORTALITY

While we may believe that we're going to die at a certain age, we also often lack urgency in relation to our lives. We live as if we have all the time in the world.

When I worked in the financial services industry, I used to ask my clients whether they would make the same decisions if they knew they only had six months to live. The reply was invariably "no." Then, I asked my clients what made them so sure that they didn't have six months left to live. None of us knows for sure how long we will live, I pointed out.

Live every day of your life as if it was your last. Don't procrastinate or you might run out of time. One of my mentors used to say that we don't have a lease on life. Don't allow yourself to arrive at the last day of your life with regrets over not achieving, or at least attempting to achieve, what you wanted.

Life is powerful but is also fragile. Our next breath could be our last. If a doctor were to tell you that unless you stopped smoking or overeating you would die within months, you'd be motivated to change your lifestyle because your perception of mortality had changed.

We need a sense of urgency to open our eyes and not take life for granted. Each of us needs to live as if our days were numbered even though we're expecting to live a long and good life. We don't have the time to postpone looking after our health and well-being if we want to achieve quality longevity.

Several years ago, I decided to do a military style HALO (High Altitude, Low Opening) parachute jump from 30,000 feet, the cruising altitude of a commercial jet. At one point during the training, the ex-military officer who was leading the group shouted at me, "Castiel, you're going to die!" I hadn't been paying attention and was questioning everything he said. I wasn't focused on the training.

We do the same thing in our daily lives. We wander away from our goals and procrastinate. Though our days may not be filled with activities as risky as leaping out of a plane, two miles high, while wearing an oxygen mask, we do need to pay attention and develop a hunger for life and the things that give us purpose, freedom, and abundance.

I have a friend who for years has been talking about getting fit and healthy. Every time I see him, he looks unhealthier. The last time I saw him, I said, "Come on, man! Don't you love yourself? Start looking after yourself."

When my children were young and I left on a business trip, I kissed them and said, "Wherever I am in the universe, I will always love you." I was conscious that I may not see them again. It's good to expect to live a long time and enjoy a wonderful life, but it is also important to break through our conditioning of complacency that tells us we are going to live forever and that everything can wait.

> When I was a boy, my father sent me to school in the United Kingdom. He told me to check it out and, if I liked it, I could stay, but if I didn't, I could return home. After being there some time, I realised that the school's ideology wasn't for me, and I didn't want to stay. When I told my father, he said that I had to tell the headmaster about my decision.
>
> The headmaster wanted to recruit other children from Gibraltar and, if I were to leave, it wouldn't be good for business. We had a long discussion in which he tried to convince me to stay. He said if I left I would never amount to anything in my life. I would always be running away from something. He was planting seeds in my mind and conditioning me for failure. I like to say he tried to put a spell on me.
>
> That sort of behaviour from a teacher or person in authority is tantamount to witchcraft if you think about it. How else can we describe someone who uses his power to influence, manipulate, and instil a negative self-belief in another person unless they comply?
>
> Fortunately, I was strong enough not to take his opinion on board and have gone on to do many positive and successful things in my life, and will continue doing so for many years to come.
>
> I often think back on that story and wonder how many children have heard something similar and lived out their life in accordance with a commandment issued to them. We all have to be vigilant to toxic conditioning and not allow it in, and especially we must protect children at all costs from any type of abuse.

CHANGE FILTERS

Another way to change limiting beliefs is to awaken to the fact that most things are invented and that we were born into an already-existing system of rules. Beliefs and social conditioning sometimes limit who we are, creating fear in our lives and holding us back.

We filter our experiences through our socially conditioned biases, and it's crucial to know where they come from. We acquire our biases and beliefs through a process of domestication. Typically, our biases come from society's invented book of rules—a dream within which we all live. It starts when we are children through the carrot and stick system—when you comply, you receive a reward; if you don't comply, you are punished.

When we grow up, we punish or reward ourselves according to how we comply with the book of rules or biases.

Every little girl or boy encounters a book of rules that includes family values, what is taught to them at school, and what they are exposed to in the outside world, such as social media, internet, and television.

The daughter of a friend of mine was bullied in school because her mother dressed in a smart and fashionable way. The other children who came from more conservative backgrounds teased her about the way her mother dressed and told her that her mother was going to die because she didn't fit in with other mothers. The little girl was scared and couldn't sleep at night.

What kind of programming did the children who bullied my friend's daughter receive? They were only seven or eight years of age and probably overheard bits of conversation from the adults around them.

Small children growing up learn that there is a "right" way and a "wrong" way to do things. Each family has its own set of beliefs. Just because we hold dear a certain belief doesn't mean that others do, or that ours is right and others are wrong. The same goes for the beliefs we've learned. Either we believe what we've been taught our entire lives, or we reach a point when we start thinking for ourselves and decide that some of our beliefs and values may no longer serve us.

We use values, beliefs, and memories as filters. They colour how we interpret our life and experiences. Like the various lenses an optician uses to test eyesight, filters affect how we see.

DELETIONS, DISTORTIONS, AND GENERALIZATIONS

We also filter information we receive by deleting, distorting, or generalizing that information.

Our brain will delete certain information from our experience. For example, when we sit in a chair, we may not be aware of the sensation of the chair on the back of our legs. Deletion reduces elements of the experience we are having in the moment that are not necessary to have in our conscious awareness. Otherwise, our conscious mind would be unable to cope with all the information coming in.

Sometimes our mind distorts what we see in front of us, like thinking a rope on the floor is a snake and then running like mad. Distortion could also occur when we are having a conversation. Sometimes we distort what we hear and unconsciously choose to take away only part of the information and ignore the rest.

Generalization occurs when we apply a specific condition to all related situations. For example, if you hired a solicitor and he cheated you, you might say that all lawyers are cheats and never hire a solicitor again. Because of your experience with one lawyer, you generalized dishonesty to all solicitors. Cheating became the filter through which you saw solicitors ever after. That's a negative application of generalization, and it's the application we use when we have biases against anything.

There is also a positive side to generalization. If you were in a foreign country, for example, you would know how to open a door because you generalized what a door is and how it works. Wherever you are, you are always able to open a door and not relearn it each time.

Programming can be good or destructive. You need to live your life as an observer and not be an open channel for everything that comes your way. Always stand guard at the gates of your mind.

CONTEMPLATIONS: QUESTIONS TO ASK YOURSELF

Please do not proceed to the next chapter until you have asked yourself the following questions and allowed yourself the time to answer them honestly. The process of transformation I present in this book depends on you doing the exercises. You might also wish to repeat these exercises in the future to discover how your life has changed.

Please write down your answers, trust what comes through, and do the exercises at the end of each chapter. Consider getting up early while the world sleeps. Taking stock and being with yourself is a way of honouring yourself. If you are able to go away for a day or two on your own, the process will be even more powerful, though it is not necessary for receiving the benefits of contemplation.

You could do the exercise on your way to work. If you

are not driving, simply close your eyes, ask yourself the questions, and write down the answers.

Whenever I choose to introspect on my life, I visualise myself in the countryside in England in a small rural village, sitting in a chapel at peace. Sunbeams flooding through the glass steeple and illuminating the inside of the chapel. I have even done this visualisation while travelling in the London subway.

1. Are you doing your absolute best?

Can you look yourself in the mirror and say that you are doing your absolute best?

When my sales team worries about having a good month, I tell them to let the month take care of itself. All they have to be concerned with is doing the very best they can in each moment and then detaching from the outcome.

By all means, have a powerful goal, but remain aware that the only thing within our control is to attempt to do our best every moment. The ultimate outcome is something we can never guarantee. All we can be sure of is the step we take each moment and do our best.

2. Are you using positive language?

Positive language is empowering. When you tell yourself that you are a coward or when you gossip about others, it will have a negative impact and bring you down.

Speak to yourself in an encouraging way, even if you are not used to it at first. Speak as if you were coaching your own child. Love and look after yourself during that process. When you do, your unconscious mind will understand and will follow suit and assist you.

3. Do you take things personally?

If you take things personally, be aware that things will fester inside you and make you unhappy, and probably sick. I believe that whatever is going on in the mind will ultimately manifest in the body.

When you catch yourself taking things personally, have a quiet word with yourself like you would with a friend or a child. Encourage yourself to stop.

4. Do you find yourself trying to read other people's minds?

Unconsciously, we make assumptions about how other people will react. We tell ourselves that we are not going to phone someone because they won't be interested in what we have to say. Those expectations are merely an invention in our mind.

When I stay in a hotel, I always ask to be upgraded to a suite, though I haven't booked one. Nine times out of ten, if the hotel has the availability, I will be upgraded. I never tell myself that it is foolish to ask for a suite because the answer will be "no."

The only way to know how anyone is going to respond is to speak directly to the person. You will never know how anyone will respond through mind reading or second guessing.

5. Do you question the context of your life?

Do you attract positive or negative situations in your life? If you are not happy with your life, you may need to change the context.

I once coached a young man who took drugs. Once he had made the decision to stop, I asked him if his friends took drugs, too. When he answered, "yes," I told him that he had to change friends. The same was true in his work environment where many colleagues took drugs, so I said that he had to change jobs. Then, he told me that he shared a house with four tenants who also consumed drugs. Obviously, I told him he had to move and live elsewhere. The only way he was going to stay off drugs for good was to change the context of his life, as hard as it may be. I am pleased to say that he trusted the process, found the boldness to make all the necessary changes and transformed his life.

Sometimes a change of context is necessary to gain a different vantage point on life.

6. Are you prepared to take massive action?

When you seek change, do you push the pendulum all the way to the other side?

If you want to change your life, it is no use changing only a little bit. You have to push the pendulum to the opposite side in order to end up in the middle. You have to be prepared to take massive action.

7. Do you argue for your potential and what is possible or do you shortchange yourself?

Never argue for your limitations or use the word "but." Never say, "I could do that, but…"

You can do anything you want. I never thought in my wildest dreams that through changing my lifestyle I would be able to cure hypertension and high cholesterol and reduce my waist size from thirty-seven to thirty-two inches. One day, I decided that I was going to do whatever it took to achieve my goal, and, over a period of a few months, I succeeded and transformed my life.

8. Are you stuck in doing and not being?

Don't confuse who you are with what you do. What you do is a process; it's a function. The more you believe that who you are is what you do, the more you are living according to your conditioning.

Observe yourself doing your daily activities versus being in your head and thinking that who you are is the activity.

If you call yourself a doctor, a carpenter, or a librarian, you are not stating who you are, but what you do. Never say I am a librarian because, unconsciously, you limit your existence to the function. Instead, say you *work as* a librarian.

9. Can you say in three or four words how another person would describe you?

Often there is a difference between how we describe ourselves and how others see us. Imagine how a person would describe you and compare it with how you describe yourself. If you are not sure, ask a couple of people who know you well to describe you. Tell them that you are reading my book and that I have requested that you ask them.

10. Who are you in order to survive in the world?

As we grow up, we have an unconscious narrative about how we are going to survive in the world. It is based on how we learned to behave in order to receive attention and reward. It's how we manipulate everything around us in order to get what we want.

Observe yourself as you go about your life. Are you still behaving today as you did as a child? Are you being who you think you should be or are you living life on your own terms and with integrity?

11. Are you living an untruth in your life?

Are you using your energy to come across as someone you are not in order to fit in?

12. Are you willing to tell yourself that you are enough?

To counter the possible negative conditioning in your life, set an alarm to go off three times a day, whether on your watch, your phone, or an alarm clock. Each time the alarm rings, say to yourself: *I am enough. I have nothing to prove to myself or others. I am whole and complete because that is the way I was created. Remember, anybody's opinion of you, including your own, is only a filtered perception of reality.*

13. **Rate yourself on a scale of one to ten—one being poor and ten being excellent—in each area of your life in order to highlight imbalances that may require attention:**

- Career
- Relationships/Social
- Financial
- Family
- Health and Fitness
- Education
- Personal Development
- Service to Community

Discuss the results with your coach or a trusted friend, or contemplate them on your own. Set goals and decide which actions you'll take, beginning immediately, to achieve balance in each area of your life that will make you happy.

For example, where do you want to be in three years' time as far as your finances are concerned? Prepare and execute a schedule of daily activities that will transport you to your financial goal in thirty-six months' time.

CHAPTER TWO

How Can You Wake Up?

THE POWER OF THE UNCONSCIOUS MIND

Our deepest fear is not that we are inadequate. Our deepest fear is that we are powerful beyond measure. It is our light, not our darkness, that most frightens us.
—MARIANNE WILLIAMSON

We store our experiences, memories, perceptions, and everything which is outside of our conscious awareness in our unconscious mind. The unconscious mind is very suggestible and the source of our conditioning.

I like to use the analogy of a filing cabinet to describe how the unconscious mind works. When we want to retrieve a document stored in a filing cabinet, we pull open the drawer and look for the document. The filing cabinet is neutral; all it does is store the information. The unconscious mind works in a similar way. It is not judgmental and doesn't know the difference between right and wrong, good and bad, or real and unreal. Its sole purpose is to store information.

Everything that has ever happened to us from the moment we left our mother's womb, and some say even whilst we were still in the womb, is stored in the unconscious mind. The unconscious mind has the capacity to hold all that we know and feel.

A number of years ago, whilst I was interviewing someone for a job, the candidate became agitated when I asked him for details about his university experience. He was fearful, and I realised that something must have happened. Later, I learned that he had been badly bullied when he was at university. It became so bad that he was driven to cut short his studies and leave. Many years after the event, his unconscious mind could not tell the difference between the reality of what was happening in the present moment while sitting in the safety of a job interview and the non-reality of a memory of aggression and danger that his unconscious mind was reliving as if it were true. The moment we spoke about university, his fear and emotions came flooding back as if he were in the original situation. He was short of breath, and his confidence collapsed.

That is an example of the way the unconscious mind works. The unconscious mind is also engaged in actions as simple as lifting an arm. Multiple muscles are involved when we lift our arm, but we don't have to consciously negotiate each muscle. Our unconscious mind does it for us, like a machine.

To illustrate how unaware we are of the unconscious mind, imagine visiting Disney World. It is summer and you are walking around, standing in lines, and enjoying the rides. You go to a restaurant and are happy with all the fun activities you have been doing. At the same time, your shoe is tight and rubbing against your ankle. Your unconscious mind is busy sending messages to your body to form a protective blister around the area. You only become aware of the irritation once the blister has formed and the pain begins. You take off your shoe and sock and see the blister. Then your conscious, logical mind redirects its attention away from the excitement of the rides to finding a bandage for your foot.

The conscious mind could be compared to the captain of a ship, and the unconscious mind to the crew. The conscious mind gives the orders, and the unconscious mind follows them. The two need one another because if the crew were not to show up, the captain would not be able to take the ship to sea. Conversely, if the crew showed up and the captain didn't, the crew would not know where to go or how to manage the journey. A captain can ask anything of the crew and they will comply. In the same way, you can ask anything of your unconscious mind, and it will comply.

> We use everything stored in our unconscious mind throughout our life.
>
> Supermarkets have back storerooms that are often four or five times larger than the store itself. It is where the shop owner stores large quantities of products for customers. Whatever the owner has stored in the back is what she is able to sell up front. If the merchandise in the back is out of date, customers will not find fresh food in the aisles of the supermarket.
>
> Similarly, whatever we have stored in our unconscious mind is what is going to fill our lives. Like the supermarket owner who stocks the warehouse with products that customers want, we have to stock the storeroom of our unconscious mind with what we want in our lives.
>
> Also, we have to refresh, or recondition, the contents from time to time. One way to refresh the contents of your mind is to go back to school and reinvent yourself. I went back to university at the age of fifty-nine to pursue a master's degree. You can also read books or attend workshops, seminars, or retreats to give yourself new ways of perceiving life and other perspectives to consider. In the process, you will meet new people, have stimulating conversations, and find your thinking transformed and rejuvenated.

THE POWER OF THE UNCONSCIOUS MIND

Very young children operate purely from their unconscious mind. They are not critical thinkers. Critical thinking is an activity of the conscious mind, which is rational, logical, and judgmental. Our programming bypasses the conscious mind and is stored in the deep recesses of the unconscious mind, only to be brought back for use at a future date. That is why children are so vulnerable to programming, and childhood is often referred to as the imprinting age.

A child does not stand guard at the gates of her mind, evaluating what to let in and what not to let in. The child's mind is like a sponge. Everything goes in, good and bad.

Little Timmy, age three, sits playing with his Legos whilst the grown-ups discuss how everyone in the family needs glasses by the age of fifteen. Timmy does not have the ability to question the truth of what they are saying, and the information passively enters his unconscious mind. The likelihood that by the age of fifteen Timmy, too, could be wearing glasses is considerable. That is how belief systems are created. Information enters our unconscious mind mostly without our being aware of it. Our ideas about how we age, succeed or fail at work, and gain or lose weight, for example, come from everything we have heard that is embedded in our unconscious mind.

The unconscious mind works in symbols and is not linear like the conscious mind. We are surrounded by symbols in life, whether in schools or institutions or from advertising, and they exert a powerful influence on our unconscious mind. They can trigger strong emotions, both positive and negative, and make us feel uncomfortable whenever we try to do things differently.

Willpower alone cannot compete with the power of the unconscious mind and the beliefs that reside there. We have to find other ways to reframe its contents so that we can succeed in the ways that we choose. We need to be in tune with our unconscious mind and speak to it in a friendly and encouraging manner, in the same sort of motivational way the captain of a ship who wants his crew to be happy and productive would communicate.

Everything that has ever been invented comes from the unconscious mind, including current technology and inventions that make the world a better place.

The source of Beethoven's Fifth Symphony came from his unconscious mind. Obviously, Beethoven had to know how to write music and used his rational conscious mind to help him achieve that, but the creativity that produced his beautiful music did not reside in his conscious mind. It was non-local.

I believe that the cosmos within us is far greater than the cosmos we see outside of us. When I was young, I was told a story that had a great impact on me. The heavenly courts were considering what to do as the human race was becoming more and more perceptive and was getting close to discovering the secret of the universe. After much discussion, one of them said, "Let's put the secret of the universe inside them. They'll never find it there." In the words of Dr. Joseph Murphy, author of *The Power of Your Subconscious Mind*, "The unconscious mind is the storehouse of infinite intelligence."

THE SUGGESTIBILITY OF THE UNCONSCIOUS MIND

The following exercise will help you appreciate the receptivity of the unconscious mind and illustrate the importance of being discerning with the information you receive, both consciously and unconsciously.

- Stand and close your eyes.
- Extend both arms in front of you and turn your palms upward.
- Imagine that someone is placing the entire thirteen-volume set of the Encyclopaedia Britannica on your left hand, one volume at a time. On the right hand,

twenty-five helium balloons are tied by a string to your fingers.
- Your left hand becomes more tired each time a heavy volume of the encyclopaedia is placed on your palm. The individual books weigh a lot and, with the addition of each one, the weight on your palm increases.
- At the same time, the helium balloons tug on your right hand. The hand gets lighter and lighter as it is pulled upwards.
- Open your eyes and look at the location of your hands. Is one hand lower and the other higher?

The likelihood is both hands have shifted position. Obviously, you did not intentionally move your hands up or down. It was the power of suggestion that caused the movement. The conscious mind had nothing to do with it, which illustrates how influential the unconscious mind is in our lives and how suggestible it is.

HAVING A CONSCIOUS RELATIONSHIP WITH YOUR UNCONSCIOUS MIND

I was once invited to appear on a television program to discuss my life and career. I was on set ten minutes before we were to go live, and I took advantage of the few minutes I had to quiet my mind and have a word with my unconscious mind. I explained to my unconscious mind that we were about to go on television, and that the outcome would be beneficial for us and for what we could do for others. I used "us" instead of "me" because I was referring to the totality of myself, including my unconscious mind. I asked my unconscious mind to help. I wanted to do well.

Then the cameras rolled. Two interviewers asked me questions for about an hour, and I have no recollection of anything I said. My unconscious mind took over. I was in a state of flow and completely aligned with my unconscious mind. The interview was a success.

My unconscious mind protected me and made sure I did well. The unconscious mind has our well-being at heart, and I had prepared it by asking for assistance while I was on TV.

Our unconscious mind will work with us on any pursuit, especially when we embrace it and create rapport with it. By asking the unconscious mind for help, we enable its creative power to come forward, work with us, and assist us as a partner. We become one with it. Be open-minded and do not let any social conditioning or limiting beliefs get in the way.

There is no limit to the amount of information the unconscious mind can hold. Try this: what's your best friend's telephone number. Where was the number before you said it? Or, what did you do and who were you with last

Christmas? Again, where was the information before you said it? It was stored in your unconscious mind.

BUILDING A RELATIONSHIP WITH THE UNCONSCIOUS MIND

In order for our unconscious mind to assist us in achieving our goals, we must give it precise instructions. If you want to weigh eighty kilos (176 pounds) by January 1, you have to give your unconscious mind the exact number of kilograms (pounds) you realistically wish to weigh and by which date. You cannot be vague. You need to be as specific as when you speak to a person.

Speak to your unconscious mind about your goal as if you have already achieved it. If you wish to weigh eighty kilos (176 pounds) by the January 1, you would say, "It is the first day of January and I weigh eighty kilos (176 pounds)."

Imagine you find yourself in San Francisco and want to travel to Paris, France. You go to a travel agent, and the first thing she asks is when you want to travel. Do you want to depart in the morning or evening? Do you wish to travel first-class or economy? Do you want a direct flight or prefer something less expensive with one or two stops? Do you need a hotel? If so, what class? Five-star or budget? Unless you give the travel agency specific instructions, how will they know what you want? It's the same with your unconscious mind.

Here is another example: if you say that you would like to come into a bit of money, you may find a dollar bill lying on the pavement, but no more. If you want to earn $10,000, you have to state the amount. You have to visualise yourself earning $10,000 in order to instruct your unconscious mind. And if you want to earn the money legally, as I trust you do, then you have to specify that as well in your instructions to the unconscious mind. (Note: We use positive language when giving our unconscious mind instructions.)

It is important that your goal is achievable. If I set a goal of winning the next Wimbledon tennis tournament and have never played tennis in my life, I would be setting myself up for failure. When I do that, the worst thing that could happen is that the next time I give my unconscious mind instructions, it probably will not believe me and may sabotage my efforts. This, in turn, could lead to undermining my self-esteem and set in motion a downward spiral of potential failures. The same thing happens in interpersonal relationships. The more unreliable I am, the less likely anyone will believe me or want to have anything to do with me. Therefore, when you say you are going to do something, do it! We have to treat our unconscious mind kindly, as we would a friend. If you show up grumpy at a meeting, who would want to work with you? You must encourage your unconscious mind like you would a colleague whom you want to motivate.

Be inclusive, work as a team, and show gratitude like the ship captain who thanks his crew at the end of a journey.

The language we use with the unconscious mind makes a difference. We must use positive language because the unconscious cannot process negative language. When we say to someone, "Don't think of a pink elephant," the first thing that pops into the person's mind is a pink elephant. Our instructions to the unconscious mind have to be presented in the positive. If you tell yourself that you cannot remember people's names, the next time you run into someone you haven't seen in a while, your unconscious mind will confirm that you never remember names, and you will not be able to recall the person's name. Instead, use an affirmation, such as, "I always remember names because I love people, and people feel good when I acknowledge them by remembering their names."

When you tell a child not to be clumsy, the focus is on clumsy, and the child has a greater likelihood of fulfilling the negative instruction. Instead, tell the child that it is okay to drop something now and then, and that it also happens to you. Help the child receive positive and constructive feedback from the experience so that she learns from situations that go wrong instead of beating herself up. Calling a child clumsy is giving them a label to walk around with for the rest of their life. I cringe when I hear parents labelling their children as shy and announcing it to the world. The child might grow up being an introvert or not find it easy to engage with other people.

Trusting in our unconscious mind is important. The unconscious mind knows more than we think it does. We have all had experiences of synchronicity when, just as we were thinking about calling a friend we haven't spoken to in a long time, the phone rings and the friend is on the line. The more recognition we give our unconscious mind, the more we'll benefit from working in partnership with it.

Because the unconscious mind follows our instructions, we need to give it directions that serve us well. We need to think twice about letting advertising determine whether we think of ourselves as happy and successful or unhappy and failing based on what they say we should be buying.

> Imagine you are walking down the street and you see a beautiful sports car entering a nearby parking space. The door opens, and out steps an eighteen-year-old driver. You wonder to yourself how a young person could drive such an expensive car. You judgmentally conclude that he either inherited the money, is into drugs, or is the son of a Mafioso.
>
> Perhaps you, too, would like to own a sports car one day, but how could it be possible if you prepare your unconscious mind in such a negative way? When it comes time to think about buying a sports car, your unconscious mind will trip you up. Your internal voice will tell you that in order to own a car like that, you have to be a crook, sell drugs, or get the money from your family; otherwise, no one like you could possibly afford a car like that. You could have created a self-fulfilling prophesy. Smile at the world and the world will smile back at you from within yourself.

ACTING AS IF

If we act like we are old, we will become old. If we act like an attractive person, people will find us attractive. When we act like we are successful, we will feel successful and be better able to align ourselves with success. If we act like we are resilient and healthy, we will want to engage in sports, go for a long walk every day, or have a session with our personal trainer. When we act as if, results will follow. Acting as if is another way of changing our social conditioning and reprogramming our unconscious mind.

I have a friend who attributes everything that happens in his life to his increasing age. As a consequence, he puts on weight, walks unsteadily on his feet, and is aging rapidly.

He has unconsciously programmed himself to become older than his years. He could have just as easily given his unconscious mind a different message and be enjoying life more fully.

COMMUNICATING WITH THE UNCONSCIOUS MIND

A good time to communicate with the unconscious mind is before going to sleep at night. Unlike the conscious mind, the unconscious mind is awake twenty-four hours a day. It heals our body, rejuvenates us whilst we sleep, and keeps our hearts pumping and our blood circulating. Show gratitude to your unconscious mind for looking after you. As part of a nightly ritual, you can ask your unconscious mind to help you prepare for the coming day. The popular expression "let me sleep on it" is, in essence, a way of providing instruction to the unconscious mind to help us work out solutions to issues we need to resolve.

CONTEMPLATIONS: QUESTIONS TO ASK YOURSELF

As you contemplate the questions below, do not overthink the answer. Trust the first thing that comes into your mind. The unconscious mind is fast. It will give you the right answer immediately, even if it surprises you. The conscious mind, on the other hand, will want to take time to think about each answer.

You can use your conscious mind to critique the responses that your unconscious mind provides. I trust my unconscious mind because I know it is giving me facts that I may not be aware of or am avoiding. However, if what comes back from my unconscious mind is a negative message, such as I am not worthy, then I pay attention and deal with it. My logical, conscious mind knows that the message is untrue because every person is born whole and complete. Something must have happened, probably when I was a child, which made my unconscious mind store the belief that I am not worthy. If I believe that to be true, even if it does not make sense, I have to change my belief or it will get in the way of my happiness and success. I begin by having a conversation with my unconscious mind, and then take massive action to succeed in life to show myself that I am worthy of success. At this stage, one may also need to consider seeing a life coach or a therapist. I believe everyone needs someone whom they trust to speak to whenever it is necessary.

CONTEMPLATIONS: QUESTIONS TO ASK YOURSELF

1. To what extent do you trust yourself?

2. To what extent would you say that you trust others?

3. Is there anything you are pretending not to know?

4. What do you want to create?

5. What do you want to learn and understand about your life?

6. What are you denying yourself?

7. Do you find yourself orchestrating your world so that you hear and see what you want?

8. What do you yearn for that you do not already have?

PART TWO

WHERE DO YOU WANT TO GO?

CHAPTER THREE

Where Are the Village Elders?

FINDING YOUR HIGHER PURPOSE AND CREATING A FAR-REACHING LEGACY

> *Where there is no vision, the people perish.*
> —KING SOLOMON

For centuries, people lived communally in villages. In those days, wisdom was passed down from one generation to the next by elders, who were held in awe and reverence. Through stories, teachings, and rituals, young people learned from adults whom they respected. Being mentored was an important part of growing up.

Some native communities around the globe still hold rites

of passage for adolescents. However, most young people today get their advice from the internet.

Contemporary families are often fragmented, and the village elders no longer exist. People rarely stay in the same town where they grew up. Young people move away to go to college, which is often far away. After graduation, they head to big cities where, typically, they live alone and remain disconnected from older generations—people in their fifties, sixties, seventies, and beyond—who could guide them through the inevitable challenges of life.

Despite technology's ability to provide us with amazing ways to communicate, many grandchildren do not take advantage of conveniences like Skype or Messenger to maintain relationships with their grandparents. At the same time, grandparents are often busy in their retirement with golf, cruises, and other activities, which contributes to the breakdown of intergenerational relationships. But without access to elders, a young person misses out on receiving heartfelt advice and wisdom from a person who has no hidden agenda and only wishes to see them thrive. Similarly, the older person also misses out on helping a young generation, as this would give them a feeling of purpose and fulfilment.

Today, young people are confronted with continuous change, but, for the most part, they are unaware of the fountain of wisdom they could turn to in times of struggle and inner conflict. They do not have time to make transitions and are expected to move from adolescence to adulthood in a single day—the day after they graduate from college.

I gave a workshop as part of a mentoring programme at Regent's University London and was surprised to hear of the sheer terror students felt when they graduated. They had no idea how to go from their lives of being cared for, which they had known since birth, to being independent and taking care of themselves. For many, it was like jumping off the edge of a cliff. Panic attacks abounded. If only they had had a group of elders to guide them, how much easier it would have been.

INTERGENERATIONAL RELATIONSHIPS

In the past fifteen years, the counselling and coaching industry has exploded. Coaching, of course, is not for young people only. Many adults well into midlife hire coaches as life can become complicated sometimes. Perhaps they did not receive the mentoring and guidance they needed as young people. Perhaps they never had a bond with a grandparent or an older person to whom they could turn for help on their road to adulthood.

When my son returned home for a break from his studies in

London, we discussed the importance of the grandchild-grandparent bond. He explained that he had not thought about it before. He decided to make a concerted effort to become closer to his grandmother (my mother). Even though he lived thousands of miles away, he started calling her regularly, and they made plans for an extended visit.

When he visited my mother, she told him stories of her life as a young woman and showed him old family photographs. She described how she had met his grandfather, who was no longer living, and the kind of person he was. Now, my son knows more of his family history, has a richer awareness of what life was like two generations ago, and has a wise and trusted person he can safely turn to for help.

An intergenerational bond requires effort from both sides. By reaching out to young people, the baby boomer and other generations have a golden opportunity to create a new paradigm of village elders. The goal is to build a meaningful relationship, not to impose one's opinions onto a young person.

Relationships are often created out of need. A person who works in sales, for example, will devote time and energy to develop a relationship with a potential client. We build relationships with our neighbours to keep the peace. But making oneself available to a young person can be viewed as an act of generosity.

By offering guidance and the insights of life experience, the older generation serves those who are starting out in life who, in turn, can be there for elders later on in their life. This encourages a repeating cycle going forward.

If you want to build a relationship and create a rapport with someone, it is important to meet the other person where they are—not expect them to meet you where you are—and show genuine interest in who they are.

THE VALUE OF PURPOSE

The baby boomer generation is different from generations that preceded it. Constituting 40 percent of the American population, boomers had a large impact on world culture with their revolutionary mindset and social activism in the 1960s. Baby boomers are living longer and are motivated to contribute to society in meaningful ways.

One great way for baby boomers to remain productive is to become a valued elder. Being an elder provides a renewed sense of purpose, a reason to stay healthy and active, and a source of happiness. To give is to be happy.

Passing on wisdom makes an impact on the future of society. When my mother speaks with my son, she doesn't give to him alone. She contributes to the well-being of her great grandchildren and to future generations whom she will never meet.

A higher purpose connects us with a panoramic view of life and life's possibilities. It reminds us of where we are going and why. Having a higher purpose helps us navigate difficult events that are irritating, painful, or frightening and saves us from becoming self-centered and selfish.

> The value of purpose should never be underestimated, as the following story powerfully demonstrates.
>
> During World War II, a group of prisoners of war in Eastern Europe were forced to push a millstone ten hours a day. All day long they could hear sounds from the nearby village, including the laughter of children playing. Their work was interminable, heavy, and hard. They were forced to toil barefoot in harsh, cold weather with their clothes in tatters. The only thing that kept the prisoners sane was their belief that the millstone was producing something of value for people in the village.
>
> When the war ended and the prisoners were freed, they discovered the millstone had no purpose whatsoever. It had simply been an instrument of torture. The prisoners were devastated because they realised there was no significance to the pain and suffering they had endured.

When I was a boy, we used to visit my grandfather in Spanish Morocco. The seas were often rough when crossing the Straits of Gibraltar to Tangier, and we had to contend with motion sickness. My mother advised us children to look out into the distant sea, giving us a focal point outside of our queasy stomachs. We would stop feeling sick she promised, and it worked.

When you discover your big "why" and project your higher purpose onto an imaginary screen in your mind—where the vision is sharp, bright, and vivid, and the sounds resonate in harmony with your purpose—the day-to-day frustrations and challenges of life will become less important. They will melt away and be dwarfed by the presence of a bigger vision.

A higher purpose will lead you to a bigger, happier, and more grounded life. You won't have to struggle or compete. Whatever actions you take in pursuit of a higher purpose will put a sweet smile on your face. They may not always be easy to carry out, but you will find creativity to help you along the way.

When you focus on what you truly want to manifest in life, you find yourself waking up each morning like a lion. I help my clients discover the treasure of having a higher purpose. It is the cornerstone of my work. Remember that Solomon the Wise said, "Where there is no vision, the people perish."

Many people work their entire lives believing that retirement will bring them the pleasure and happiness they seek. When they finally stop working, they quickly learn that a life focused on pleasure alone feels aimless and boring, particularly if they don't have a pre-existing network of friends and activities. Lassitude takes over. It is a fine art to balance pleasure and purpose and requires deliberate attention and intention.

Purpose steers our life. I remember a time in my life when I couldn't find my purpose. It was like sitting in a rudderless boat in the middle of a dark ocean. I didn't know how far I was from the shore, or how I would find my way back home. I grasped at straws and got involved in ventures that didn't serve me.

Purpose creates stability and sustainability. As your purpose grows, so will you, and you will have a positive impact on the planet.

Purpose can be many things. It could be writing a book to influence others about a way of living, one that will empower them and make their life better. It could involve building a business, a charity, or a family. You could engage in an activity that makes you feel like a world citizen. Helping a neighbour can bring a sense of purpose to life, as can forging an authentic, meaningful bond with children and grandchildren, as I discussed above.

A major obstacle to finding purpose is fear of commitment. Goethe said it beautifully:

"Until one is committed, there is hesitancy, the chance to draw back, always ineffectiveness. Concerning all acts of initiative (and creation), there is one elementary truth, the ignorance of which kills countless ideas and splendid plans: that the moment one definitely commits oneself, then Providence moves too."

MY PURPOSE

My purpose, along with being an elder to my children and future grandchildren, is to help people tap into their greatness. For as long as I can remember, my goal has been to help people reshape their lives through transformational thinking.

Too many people have been programmed since childhood to align with the weakest part of themselves—the villain that holds us back. We can all stimulate change in others, in small ways and large, whether it's through listening to the stories of the person sitting next to us on an airplane or recommending a book to a taxi driver, like I once did in New York City. (The book I recommended was Napoleon Hill's *Think and Grow Rich*. The taxi driver immediately stopped the car and went into Barnes and Noble to buy the book, while I waited in the taxi. He was so hungry for success that he didn't want to waste another moment. I encourage people everywhere to read it if you haven't done so already.)

Another important purpose in my life is the pursuit of freedom. That is why I left a secure job with a final salary pension scheme in the City of London and returned to Gibraltar to start my own business. Initially, I paid my dues and sold books door to door for two years, which was soul-destroying at times, before I was able to humbly launch my financial services company. I grew my company in a few years, and it became the leading homegrown financial services company in Gibraltar. I went on to sell it and became financially independent.

Millions of people are happy working in the corporate world, but I was not. Living my dream of owning a business was too important for me. I was fully prepared to pay the price and take the risks to acquire my freedom.

Purpose fuels perseverance and boldness.

At one point, I was trying to do business with a large transportation company in Gibraltar. They had a big staff and were in the market for a corporate pension scheme. For months, I had been unable to secure an appointment with the CEO. Every time I called the office, his personal assistant told me he was busy. She said she would call me back when he was free, but she never did. I wasn't the only person in Gibraltar who received this treatment. Everyone who wanted to do business with him had the same experience.

One day, I phoned and spoke to the secretary again. I asked for a brief appointment in the afternoon, but she said that was impossible because the CEO would be on the British Airways flight to London in a few hours.

I hung up the phone, left the office, and went home to pack a bag. When my wife asked me where I was going, I replied, "To London." She wanted to know why. "I'll tell you later," was all I had time to say to her.

I dashed to the airport. I knew the CEO would be travelling business class, so I bought a business-class ticket. Fortunately, I had friends at the airport who kindly arranged for me to sit next to him.

The CEO and I travelled to London together. I had his uninterrupted attention for two hours, which we spent conversing about many things. When we arrived in London, he invited me to his home for dinner and eventually gave me the go-ahead to set up a pension scheme for his company. It was the most lucrative piece of business I had ever written to that point. We became great friends and did business together thereafter.

One of the biggest lessons I learnt in life is that when you have a purpose, you innovate rather than compete. I have never really competed for anything. Instead, I look for the creative solution, which is staring me in the face most of the time, and implement it.

A competitive advantage comes from the fact that most people prefer the status quo and obvious solution. If my purpose had been that I would only have succeeded in sales under the condition that everything went smoothly and opportunities presented themselves to me on a silver platter, I wouldn't have found success. I had faith in myself and the boldness to back up my purpose in order to succeed under any circumstances.

I believe that we either get the result we want, or we make an excuse for not getting it. I once coached a young person who wasn't doing well in university. We identified that his fear of failure was causing him to not study or prepare his assignments. Paradoxically, he believed that by not doing the work, he would not have to face potential failure. Have you ever experienced something similar?

THE POWER OF COMMITMENT

Purpose, goals, and motivations are inextricably linked. When I was building my financial services business, I sold life insurance and pension schemes, among other services, but I didn't see it as my purpose. My purpose was (1) to protect families from financial hardship if the breadwinner died, and (2) to help clients make financial decisions that would provide for them as they entered old age, so they could enjoy sandy beaches in the summertime and mittens in the wintertime. That was my incentive for finding clients. If I had been focused only on making money, I would not have been successful. My motivation drove my goals, which were aligned with my purpose—to make families financially healthy.

Whenever we are aligned with our values we find purpose, which is the foundation of a happier, more meaningful life. One of the biggest stumbling blocks, as it is in other areas of life, is the fear of commitment. Without commitment, we will never be successful or fulfil our purpose. In addition to fearing commitment, many of us struggle with procrastination.

One way to work with these twin challenges is to make a plan. If you were travelling to a foreign country, you would plan your journey in advance. You wouldn't just jump into the ocean and try to swim to your destination. Having a plan helps overcome obstacles.

Before you go to bed at night, think about the five most important actions you want to accomplish the following day. Rank them in order of priority. If you can't complete everything on your list, at least you will have accomplished the most important tasks. Then, you can go to bed knowing you have taken care of tomorrow. Your unconscious mind will be more relaxed, and you will sleep better.

If you wake up in the morning without a plan, your time will not belong to you. You'll squander it or someone else will borrow it. People who are busy look for people who aren't and ask them to do errands or chores.

Prioritizing creates focus. It helps sort out what deserves attention from what doesn't, whether it relates to health, exercise, work, or relationships. We tend to lose much of our life energy by not taking the time to plan and prioritize our activities.

Prioritizing doesn't take much time. All it requires is a commitment to yourself. I recommend setting aside ten to fifteen minutes at the same time each day to spend prioritizing. When you develop the habit of prioritizing every day, you create structure and momentum. By investing a small amount of time, you are better focused, can plan for the day ahead, and will feel less anxious.

I built a successful company by staying focused when adversity reared its head.

One afternoon, about two years after I had established my firm, I was waiting for a client to arrive when my assistant rushed into my office. She told me that a government official was in the waiting room and needed to speak with me immediately about an urgent matter.

The official told me he was a building inspector and that we had to evacuate the building at once because it was in danger of collapsing. Whilst working on one of the shops on the ground level, construction workers had mistakenly removed a support beam.

I thought I was on the television programme, *Candid Camera*. When I realised the building inspector was serious, I told him that I couldn't possibly leave right away. I had a meeting scheduled with a client. He replied by saying that the danger was so extreme that if I didn't leave immediately, he would have to call the police to evict me.

Suddenly, I was locked out of my place of business! I had no access to client files, and I couldn't reach the landlord. I chased him high and low and finally tracked him down at an event at his children's school.

Reluctantly, the landlord agreed to pay for the cost of a small room at the local Holiday Inn so that I could move my entire office. We packed everything into that tiny space and connected the phone lines. My wife painted a sign that said our company had moved to Room 106 of the Holiday Inn, and I climbed the scaffolding of the weakened building to nail it near the entrance.

A few days later, accompanied by a couple of labourers whom I had hired, I entered the building at four o'clock in the morning when no police were around, removed our filing cabinets and took them to our temporary office at the Holiday Inn. I felt I had a responsibility to my clients and was willing to risk getting into trouble with the police in order to honour it and save my business. In financial services, especially in the days before computers, if you didn't have client files, you were no longer in business.

We continued doing business out of our small hotel room as if nothing had happened. Six months later, I was blown away when I received an investment of half a million pounds whilst still ensconced in that tiny office at the Holiday Inn. By the time another six months had passed and the building had been reinforced, allowing us back into our offices, our business had doubled in size from the previous year.

I didn't let a temporary problem put us out of business or set the business back. On the contrary, it gave us the reason to flourish and go beyond our wildest expectations. I was determined to become the leading financial services firm in Gibraltar. I always kept that panoramic view at the forefront of my mind.

Irrespective of adversity, if you have a purpose and a big "why" for life, nothing between heaven and earth can stop you from fulfilling your dream. Our fears and limitations are inventions of our mind. When we have purpose and determination, we can walk step-by-step through any challenges to achieve success.

THE DVD OF YOU™

Visualization is a powerful tool for manifestation. One helpful exercise I like to teach in my workshops is what I call The DVD of You™.

Imagine that you are putting a DVD into the DVD player. The story that appears on the screen is the story of your life as it exists now—everything that you are doing and creating. Then you fast-forward the DVD and look at your life in three, five, and ten years' time. What do you see at each junction? Do you like what you're seeing? Do you want to see yourself doing exactly what you are doing today magnified many times over in the future?

Consider, for example, that you are in an abusive relationship, one that is destroying your life. What will your life be like ten years from now if you don't take massive action to change your circumstances? *The DVD of You*™ can help you see into the future and find the motivation to transform your circumstances *now*. But it will take guts, courage, and honesty to be able to watch *The DVD of You*™ in your imagination.

My father would have been in a much better physical state the last ten to fifteen years of his life if he had watched a DVD of himself and been motivated to become fit and healthy. I applied *The DVD of You*™ exercise to my life and saw that my health was going to end up the same as my father's if I didn't transform my lifestyle to include healthier habits, such as working out, eating nutritious foods, and losing weight.

None of us are here on planet Earth without a reason. We are here to create. Every one of us, like Nature herself, is always in a state of becoming. A flower or a tree never gets depressed; they don't ruminate on what happened yesterday or worry about tomorrow. They simply grow, are present, and bring beauty into the world.

We, too, can grow and progress as individuals, like a flower or a tree, at the pace that is perfect for us. What we must never do is give ourselves excuses for stagnating and not moving forward. When you are not progressing in any field of endeavour, you go backwards, against the natural flow of the universe. Nature always moves forward and grows; the cycle never stops.

VISUALIZATION EXERCISE FOR CREATING YOUR FUTURE

Create an image and visualize the most vivid manifestation of what you want your life to be.

Imagine you can control the colour, contrast, brightness, and volume of what you see and hear.

Now play with the controls until you optimize the vision and the sounds you want to see and hear. Hold the image between your hands and, as you look at it, see yourself in it. Exhale three warm breaths onto the image in order to really bring it to life.

Now bring the image with you and imagine that you've flown out of your head and are travelling into the future. Decide where the image belongs and drop it there.

Now, as if you were looking through a time tunnel, look back from where you dropped the image and notice how all the events in your life have changed. They are now supporting the new life you just created.

Then travel back to now, knowing that through this visualization you have taken responsibility for your life and created your future.

I refer to this visualization technique elsewhere in the book. It can be used to manifest your goal, whatever the context.

Remember, everything is in a state of becoming. When we move forward, the Universe moves with us. If life is about growth—and I believe it is—this might be a good time to ask yourself, "What is next for me?"

CONTEMPLATIONS: QUESTIONS TO ASK YOURSELF

In order to discover your higher purpose—the big "why" of your life—you need to know that you can thoroughly depend on yourself.

Take time to ask yourself the following questions before you proceed to the next chapter.

1. Are you truthful with yourself?

If, in the area of health and fitness, for example, you tell yourself that everything is fine whilst you are on medication, not exercising, eating the wrong food, and not doing what the doctor tells you, how can everything be fine?

You would be lying to yourself and doing nothing to resolve your problems. You would not be honouring yourself. You would be undermining your self-esteem and, most importantly, you would lose confidence and belief in yourself.

Would you trust someone who lies to you on a regular basis and treats you like an idiot?

Now, ask yourself the question again, are you truthful with yourself, in the context of the other areas of your life:

- Career/Business
- Relationships/Social
- Financial
- Family
- Health and Fitness
- Education
- Service to Community
- Personal Growth and Development

2. Are you aware of your values, your belief system, and the agreements that you have made with yourself? Do they serve and empower you, or do they detract and belittle you?

We acquire our values and belief system as we grow up. Everything you encounter in life is filtered through how you were programmed by your environment, your parents, your teachers, and society. None of us experiences life purely and directly. We experience life through what we have learned—what I refer to as our biases and invented notions.

Observe yourself and become aware of your biases as you experience them. Work out where they came from. Become your own case study and have fun with it.

It is crucial for your unconscious mind to understand that most of your beliefs about yourself are invented, especially when they limit your confidence and progress. You are on a quest to expose the lie that you are not enough or not worthy of love so you can reach the summit, stick your flag in the ground, and claim your personal power. That is the journey to loving yourself, being proud of yourself, and believing in yourself.

3. When you are on your deathbed, what incomplete projects will haunt you? Who would you make peace with? What about the book you never wrote, your dream to circumnavigate the world you never fulfilled, or the time you never took to develop a relationship with your child or grandchild in order to impact future generations? If you knew you had six months to live, what would you do right now and how do you know you don't have six months to live?

Our mortality is a great motivator. Don't let fear, procrastination, or disorganization keep you from doing the things that truly matter.

The motivational speaker Les Brown said,

> Imagine if you were on your death bed—And standing around your bed—the ghosts of the ideas, the dreams, the abilities, the talents given to you by life. And that

for whatever reason, you never acted on those ideas, you never pursued that dream, you never used those talents, we never saw your leadership, you never used your voice, you never wrote that book. And there they are, standing around your bed looking at you with large angry eyes saying we came to you, and only you could have given us life! Now we must die with you forever. The question is—if you died today, what ideas, what dreams, what abilities, what talents, what gifts, would die with you?

4. If you found yourself in heaven and were offered a second chance in life, would you take it? What would you do differently?

Perhaps you would take better care of your body and look after your health and fitness, or take time to develop good relationships with your loved ones. Maybe you would learn more, go back to university, learn a language, or decide not to sweat the small stuff. As Richard Carlson said in his book *Don't Sweat the Small Stuff*, it's all small stuff.

The fact is, at this moment, you are not dead and not in heaven, and you can make all the changes you want here and now. You have the rest of your life in front of you, so take massive action today. Why wait and hope for a second chance? Your chance is now!

5. How do you deal with disappointment? Do you take things personally? Do you hang onto things? Do you allow things to fester and become toxic inside?

If you do, it is bad for your mental and physical health.

Secondly, when you live like that, you are never in the here and now where everything is usually fine. We jump from thought to thought like a monkey jumping from branch to branch. When we do, we are not truly living life. Life only happens in the present.

Whenever you live with resentment, you are living in your head—reliving some event that doesn't serve you and probably continues to torment you and affect your physical and mental health. Let go of gnawing thoughts you are holding onto and listen to the sounds that are happening around you. The sounds you hear are in the present moment. Use those sounds as your trail back to now, where you know all is well.

I recommend that you cultivate the boldness to have a peaceful and powerful conversation with the person or people with whom you have a problem. Be truthful about how you feel. Get the toxicity out of your system.

6. Do you fight for what is important to you?

If you do, that is fantastic. If you don't, ask yourself about the message you are sending to your unconscious mind. What is so important to you that you don't fight for? What are you settling for by not fighting? Are you accepting the crumbs when you are entitled to the whole loaf of bread? Where did you learn that you should act in this way?

Replace your unwholesome and disempowering agreements with agreements which empower you and serve you. You deserve the best, provided it is legal and doesn't harm another.

7. Do you defend or stand up for what you believe in?

In the same way as exercising, you build inner strength by honouring yourself and taking every opportunity to defend and stand up for what you believe in.

8. What do you yearn for?

Many of us find ourselves yearning for something more in our lives, but we don't take the time to find out what it is. Sometimes the yearning quietly hides in the background and doesn't have an opportunity to manifest itself.

By taking time for yourself and questioning what you yearn for, you uncover clues that help you find your purpose and happiness. You honour and respect yourself when you do, and you boost self-esteem and self-love.

9. When was the last time you were motivated and excited?

We become busy with work, commitments, and raising a family. Before we know it, we hit a glass ceiling because our baggage is so heavy. We yearn for more, but we don't know how to reach it. We stagnate, lose our motivation, feel bored, and hate the monotony in our lives.

When this happens, I suggest you go back to basics and embark on a journey of discovery. Consider the activities you loved when you were ten years old, fifteen, twenty-five, thirty-five, and so on. Look for patterns that motivated you, made you happy, and gave you purpose and fulfilment. Revisit those activities, whether it was joining a club or singing in a choir. Learn to play an instrument. Bake a cake. Volunteer to help others or the planet. Wherever you begin, you will see your motivation grow and opportunities come your way through the law of attraction.

10. Are you prepared to give up your old story—the constant thought that holds you back? What would you commit to accomplishing if you knew nothing could stop you?

Nothing more than a thought holds you back. If you need to learn something new in order to move on, all you have to do is go back to school or study through an online course.

If you need to become a fitter and healthier person, all you need to do is get a personal coach or attend a fitness class. If you are unhappy with your job, all you have to do is start searching for a better opportunity. Don't allow the villain inside to talk you out of anything and lead you into the tunnel of procrastination or the bridge to nowhere. Take massive action now!

11. Are you prepared to let go of the things that no longer serve you?

12. List ten things you would do if you had no fear.

As you accomplish each item on the list, take pleasure in placing a big tick across it.

Psychologists say that babies are born with only two fears: the fear of falling and the fear of loud noises. To me, that means that all other fears are learned. If we can learn them, we can unlearn them. Be gutsy.

CHAPTER FOUR

Are You the Hero of Your Own Journey?

YOUR KEY TO TRANSFORMATION

A person is limited only by the thought that he chooses.

—JAMES ALLEN

The villain within represents doubt and procrastination, whereas the hero within represents your innate power to do battle and win.

When I was a young man working for a property developer in London, my life looked like it was set in stone. I was lined up for a final-salary pension scheme, which would have paid me two-thirds of my final salary for the rest of my life upon retirement. I had a company car, along with a path to top management and a possible directorship. Then, as I mentioned earlier in the book, I made the decision to leave the job and return to Gibraltar to start my own business.

When I was back in Gibraltar, I realised I didn't yet have a good idea for a business of my own, so I took a commission-based job selling educational books door-to-door. I could have snubbed that low-paying, heart-wrenching job, especially having come from a posh job in the City of London, but I needed money to pay my bills. I didn't want to squander the savings for starting a business I had managed to set aside over many years. I had burned my bridges behind me and made the leap.

Sometimes more is required than simply crossing a bridge. You have to burn the bridge down so that you corner yourself in a position you can't easily escape to keep you from settling for mediocrity. I was a door-to-door salesman for three years, and it taught me that in order to transform my life, I had to pay my dues.

At one point, I realised that part of the world was awake at night, and I didn't have to depend only on private residences for sales. People worked through the night at fire stations, police stations, hospitals, port offices, security companies, and other businesses. I transformed my situation and doubled my income by calling on them. Indeed, people welcomed me because things were quiet at night, provided there were no emergencies.

Soon, people started talking about the crazy book salesman who worked through the night, which led to an insurance brokerage firm offering me a job selling life insurance on commission. This, in turn, led to starting my own business a few months later from humble beginnings.

My business went from strength to strength and eventually became the leading home-grown financial services firm in Gibraltar. Our clients included international corporations and banks, as well as thousands of private clients. Half of the working population of the city were clients. I laugh when I think about it now because years prior, before I had a job in property development in London, I had been told by an insurance company that they wouldn't hire me because I didn't have the right character for selling life and disability insurance. They told me I wouldn't succeed.

That experience taught me that you can never let someone's opinion of you become your reality. You must believe in what's in front of your eyes and stay in the present moment. That is where you'll find the tools you need for transformation, whatever they may be.

TAKE THE ROAD LESS TRAVELLED

Leaving my good job in London was not the only thing I left behind. Maxine, the woman in my life, had a great job as a fashion designer. I was torn between the risk of losing her and pursuing my destiny.

With the benefit of hindsight, I know what would have happened if I had stayed in London. The first year, I would have continued doing well in my job and been appreciated by my employers. Maxine and I would have continued having fun and planning our future. The second year, my unconscious mind would have reminded me of the destiny I wanted to pursue, even though I would be convincing myself that I was doing the right thing. A year or so later, knowing deep down that I wasn't pursuing my dream for freedom, I would have had difficulty sleeping at night. Maxine would have sensed my frustration and unhappiness and felt partly to blame. Finally, four or five years later, after having taken on the commitments of children and a mortgage, I would no longer be concerned about my destiny. I would have lost the ability to read the signs that appear in all of our lives to motivate us to pursue a life of purpose, freedom, and abundance.

Maxine may have been young at the time, but she was wise and understood that I was looking for my treasure. She let me go with her blessings and a big smile, knowing that decision would keep me from settling for an unfulfilled life of mediocrity. We took a risk and trusted that one day, once I had found my treasure, we would be reunited.

Transformation is about taking a quantum leap. It is tantamount to alchemy, in which base metal is converted into gold. To change means altering what we do, while transformation involves changing who we are. Positive thinking alone is not enough to create transformation, although it helps. When I left London, I was not merely leaving a job and hoping things would turn out for the better. I pursued my destiny and passed through a threshold of life as I journeyed forward.

I had a higher purpose and searched for who I truly was. I sensed that what I had experienced in my life was only the tip of the iceberg of what was possible for me.

We all have to become explorers in our lives and have the boldness, like the ancient mariners, to set off from a safe harbour in search of our destiny, irrespective of our age and stage in life. We have to watch for signs and become sensitive to what life is telling us. We have to develop our sensory acuity and intuition, knowing that it will guide us through challenges and opportunities, and recognize that our decisions will transport us to a life beyond our present circumstances. If we don't have the courage to make decisions, we will remain stuck in limbo. I agree with Albert Einstein when he said that a ship is always safe at the shore, but that is not what it is built for.

It is important to reframe how you view your life, instead of complaining or feeling bitter. Become aware that you are on a sacred journey of discovery and that everything is in a state of becoming, including yourself.

The posh company I worked for in London eventually went out of business, so it was a good thing that I listened to what life was urging me to do. Maxine and I built a wonderful life together, and I have pursued and found many treasures in my life. I am now in a new and exciting stage in the journey of my life, where I bring the jewels I have discovered and gathered. Every time we enter a new stage in our journey of life we bring with us the wisdom and experiences from previous stages. To believe that one must stop creating because of age is a waste of what we can do with that treasure. We all have so much to bring into the world, and I will keep forging ahead until my last breath.

A quantum leap can happen in an instant. We must remain vigilant to the opportunities that we attract by the seeds we sow, so that our lives can be transformed. We need guts and boldness to seize the moment and act when opportunities arrive. Transformation does not depend on circumstances or timing. It depends entirely on you and what you think. The decisions you make are the channels to your future.

Some years ago, my wife Maxine was on the verge of needing insulin injections three times a day. She was diabetic; her sugar levels were out of control, and she potentially faced a lifetime of insulin dependency. Standing on the edge of a precipice, Maxine decided to transform her life. She hired a personal trainer and started regularly working out. She completely altered her diet and lost weight. Three months into her new regime, her doctor said she didn't need insulin. She only had to take a pill once a day. My wife's story is one of transformation.

Transformation can happen in small steps, too. If you want to lose weight, start by giving up sugar, potatoes, pasta and bread for twelve weeks. Go for a brisk thirty minute walk everyday. Adopt the habit of drinking eight glasses of water per day and know that drinking lots of water is good for you. Then see what happens after twelve weeks.

A simple conversation with someone you meet on the street could be transformative, and you could never be the same person again. Stay aware and value the seemingly small events in your life.

If you choose to climb Mount Everest, do it one step at a time. Each step will be a search for who you are at that particular point in your journey. You will transform your life by paying attention and being fully present. Your life will never be boring, and you will be fulfilled by living with purpose.

A PILOT'S TRUST

The story of American pilot Chesley Burnett "Sully" Sullenberger III is an unforgettable one. In 2009, he safely landed a commercial passenger aircraft on the Hudson River in the middle of Manhattan in New York City. The plane had encountered a flock of birds shortly after take-off, and several of them got caught in the plane's engines. The plane quickly lost power and altitude, but thanks to Sullenberger's quick thinking, the lives of 155 passengers and five crew members were saved. He transformed a hopeless situation that promised impending death into one of life.

Trust made the difference for Sullenberger. He had confidence in his ability to land the plane on the river. A fraction of a second off and the plane would have been destroyed. He understood that the passengers' safety depended on him, and that there were no guarantees. Transformation often comes when we have the stillness of mind to stand between two thoughts and do the right thing by utilizing everything we've learned and experienced up to that precise moment.

We must remain aware that we have everything at our disposal to take the next step, whether it involves learning a new skill or going back to university, like I did at the age of fifty-nine. We need to trust our life trajectory and listen to what life is telling us. But always be careful! The voice inside your head could be the villain within, trying to put you off, trying to make you procrastinate.

Your choices may make you feel uncomfortable. Like being in the gym and lifting weights, you may come up against the resistance of your habits and programming, and your decisions could keep you awake at night. That is what happened to me when I decided to skydive out of a plane from 30,000 feet, the cruising altitude of a commercial jet. Before I could do it, I had to work on myself and go boldly where I had never been before. We often have to raise the bar in order to stay in the game and not resign ourselves to lives of mediocrity and boredom, with all their unpalatable consequences.

RESPONDING VERSUS REACTING

Consider those times when you have had a disagreement with someone. If you reacted, the situation probably became more painful and difficult to resolve. When you get out of your mind and are present, you are able to respond and not react. You create space and are able to watch your next thought being born.

By responding to life's situations instead of reacting, you prevent emotional baggage from entering your conversations. You can watch the situation instead of being consumed by it. When you are awake in the here and now, you can lead the disagreements to rational, peaceful conclusions without involving the emotions. That is a quantum leap in transformation, especially if you normally react emotionally without thinking. There will likely always be one person or subject matter that will push your buttons and cause you to lose your composure. When that happens, you will have to work harder to stay present and not allow the monkey in your head to take over.

EXPECT THE BEST

Our ability to be in the here and now and expect the best leads to transforming a potentially challenging situation into a good outcome. Perhaps you are heading to the office one morning to meet an important client who is a grumpy person and doesn't like to be kept waiting. You get in your car, and it doesn't start. You keep turning the ignition and become increasingly more upset and flustered. Your heart beats faster, you start to perspire, and on the screen of your mind, you imagine the worst possible outcome—you lose the account, your job, and your house (our imaginations are the best screenwriters!).

The way forward is to get out of your mind and find refuge

in the here and now so that you can be calm and respond appropriately to the situation. You call the office and ask your assistant to explain the situation to the client and reschedule the appointment. You offer to take your client out to lunch to compensate for wasting his time. Your creative juices flow when you are in the here and now, and you are not kidnapped by your mind and your emotions. You change your relationship to what is happening and, in so doing, transform your day. If Sullenberger had not responded to his situation by staying calm, expecting the best, and being fully present, who knows what would have happened.

Earlier in the book, I talked about how we tend to put endless energy and emotions into regurgitating the stories about our past and future that run through our heads. Staying in the present and keeping calm is the alternative to those stories and frees our energy so that we can transform.

Most of us live in our heads, and our minds never rest. There is no reprieve, not even for a split second. We live out all our thoughts about the past and the future, even though most of them are figments of our imagination.

Most people don't know how to escape their minds. They believe that they and their minds are the same thing. When you dis-identify from your mind, you find your presence.

Transformation is about simplicity. Life does not have to be complicated, but we often make it so. Many people suffer from Monday-morning syndrome on Sunday evening. They dread the thought of going to work the next day instead of enjoying their Sunday. They are kidnapped by the stories they run in their mind.

We all need to find paradise. Paradise is found in the present moment. It is always within you. To help yourself be in the here and now, you may need to set an alarm to to bring you back at different times of the day. Normally, everything is fine in the present moment. When you think about the past or wish to plan for the future, do so from the refuge of the here and now and remove the stress.

THE POWER OF THE PRESENT

I wrote that transformation can happen in a moment, but it can also take longer. Think of the caterpillar in the chrysalis. It takes time for the caterpillar to complete metamorphosis and turn into a butterfly.

It is not uncommon for people who are undergoing a process of transformation to feel like they are stuck. Here again, having trust is critical. You will reach the other shore, even though it feels like you are trapped in the middle of the ocean at night.

We already know that we are in a process of transformation in the same way that nature is. We never see a flower suffer from depression, feel unfulfilled, or not know where it is headed. The flower has internalised its own potential and so grows, turns into something of beauty, and is in a state of flow with the universe. When we don't act like the flower, we move against that flow. We stop loving ourselves and are unfulfilled. Boredom sets in and depression and anxiety take over.

Everything is created in the present moment. That is why the present moment is a holy, sacred, and powerful moment. For creation to be sustainable, it must take place in the here and now, not the past. The force of life itself is present in everything. Therefore, I believe that the universe is intelligently created every second. If not, we would disappear into oblivion.

TAKE REFUGE IN THE PRESENT MOMENT

When we find our minds racing from one thought to another, like a monkey leaping from branch to branch, we have a choice. We can escape the craziness of our lives and our overly active minds by going to a place of refuge. We can become completely present.

When we do, we not only give our minds a reprieve and a sense of peacefulness, we are also kind to our bodies. Our minds and our bodies heal when we come back to the present moment. Think about it this way: we are told that when we are asleep at night our bodies repair and heal. Why do you think that is? You see, our conscious mind is not getting in the way of our healing with its incessant internal dialogue regarding worries of the future and resentments of the past.

Here are some simple tools you can use that will help remind you how to wake up to the here and now:

- Listen to the sounds around you. Those sounds are in the here and now. As you listen to the sounds, you are not thinking about what is going to happen tomorrow or later in the day. You are fully present with the sounds. The more you practice this exercise, the more you will be able to stay with the sounds and be present for longer periods of time. You can easily do this exercise wherever you happen to be, even while walking down the street.

- When you get into your car, take a few moments before you turn on the ignition. Look at the steering wheel or the gear stick, or smell the interior of the car. Become conscious of the feeling of the seat pressing against your back. The steering wheel, the gear stick, the smell, and the sensation of the seat against your back are all happening in the now. Stay with the sensations, and you will get out of your head and wake up in the now.

- Locate and become aware of your body. Your body occupies space in the here and now. When you are aware of your body rather than the thoughts in your head, you are fully present. The here and now is the only reality. Life happens and is created in the now. Every moment is a new now. Whenever you think of something that will take place in the future, it is just a figment of your imagination, as it hasn't happened yet.

- Breathe. You can only breathe now. That is where life happens and nowhere else. Become aware of your in-breath and your out-breath. Stay with your breath and be in the present moment.

- Instead of using a dishwasher, at least once a week wash your dishes by hand. Feel the warm water and soap running through your fingers as you hold a plate. See how shiny and clean the plates are once they are washed.

- Notice and feel. Everything you experience through your senses is in the here and now. You are fully present and your mind is at rest from the incessant roller coaster of thoughts. When you consciously experience something through your five senses, you take yourself out of your mind and the world of thought, and you wake up in the now. Even if it is just for a few moments, you live in the only reality there is, a place of refuge and calm.

- Take refuge in each of your steps. As you walk down the street, become aware of the ground pressing up against the soles of your feet each time you take a step and know that that is happening in the now. Look at the faces of the people you pass on the pavement and know that those people are in the present moment with you.

- Be present with the people in your life each time you're with them. Being mindful of the present moment helps you focus and be effective in every area of life. Imagine how you will improve your personal or professional relationships when you are fully present with people. They might not know what has happened to you, but they will certainly sense that they are receiving a level of attention from you that they have never experienced before.

- Be aware of your own physical existence. When you look out from behind your eyes, it is like looking out of a window. Everything you see is in the here and now, the only place where you and reality exist. Everything outside of the here and now resides in your imagination. Maintaining this awareness will transform your life. When I discovered this truth, it was like finding a palatial room in my house that I didn't know existed.

REINVENT YOUR LIFE

When I was eleven years old and going to school in Gibraltar, we had to take an exam that determined our future educational trajectory. If we passed, we went to an academic school that prepared students for university. If we failed, we went to a less academic school. It was a cruel exam because not only did it determine at a young age the type of education a student would receive, it also defined one's life. I did not pass the exam.

From the age of thirteen, I worked all of my school holidays as a labourer in a laundry. While my friends went to the beach every day during the summer, I only went on Sundays. I saved as much money as I could. After graduating from high school, I found a job in sales. A year later, I left for London in search of my fortune. I was nineteen at the time and had been raised in a small city where everyone knew everyone else. London was frighteningly enormous.

I persevered in London and found a job as the manager of a two-story menswear store in King's Road, Chelsea, one of London's hippest fashion streets. The street was the centre of punk culture in those days. I was twenty and managing people twice my age. I don't know how I managed to convince them to give me the job. I remember my uncle, a professional actor, saying to me when I was growing up, "Always act the part, and if you are good enough, people will believe you." Perhaps that was the reason. Of course, I delivered with flying colours and worked hard.

Four years later, I was back in Gibraltar, working as a buyer and manager of a high-end jewellery business, and one night I happened to find my brother's university course catalogue lying on the table. He is five years younger than me and was preparing to go to university. It was late, but I started looking through the catalogue and found a course in business administration that caught my eye.

I daydreamed and wondered what it would be like to be in university and learn exciting business concepts. In glancing through the course descriptions, I realised that I had five years of practical experience in the business world. I also knew that I had missed my chance of going to university when I failed the exam at age eleven. I went to sleep with a disappointed heart.

By morning, I had secretly decided to leave my job and go to university. Nothing between heaven and earth was going to stop me. I phoned the university, which was located in Bournemouth in the United Kingdom, and spoke to the programme director of the course I was interested in. I told him what I had done with my life up until then. I explained that I didn't have the proper high school qualifications because I had failed the eleven-plus exam, but I did have five years of management experience and a strong work ethic. I also explained that, since the age of thirteen, I had been saving money to go to school. I would be happy to send him a copy of my bank statement to prove that I could pay my way.

He obviously heard in my voice the hunger for an education and replied in proper Queen's English, "That won't be necessary, old chap. It will be my pleasure to make you an offer to study with us straight away. Just send me some work references and that will be sufficient. We need more people like you—mature students who can positively influence our younger students and show them how to win at life." Before hanging up, he added, "And by the way, old chap, regarding the eleven-plus exam, it's a load of codswallop, so don't spare another thought over it."

Not long thereafter I found myself in the UK, sitting in a huge lecture hall with hundreds of nineteen-year-old students, wondering what the hell had I done! I was twenty-four at the time and had just turned my life upside down, but sometimes that is exactly what we need to do in order to move forward and make progress.

Because of my early schooling, I was convinced that I was no good at studying and would never amount to anything academically. It didn't take me long at university to realise that I was better at studying than I thought I was. My work ethic helped me, too, to achieve top results, and I completed my studies with distinction. On my last day of class as I was walking down the stairs after my final exam, I made a vow never to allow circumstances to determine what I was capable of achieving. I committed to succeeding in life, including financially, by taking full responsibility for my results. No exam at the age of eleven, or anything else for that matter, would ever get in my way again.

I always remember a story I heard about a young boy who was being bullied by some older boys on a bus. While they held him down on the floor, he wrestled and shouted at them, "You may be holding me down, but I'm standing up inside of me."

That's the spirit which carries you to the highest pinnacles of life.

I paid for university out of my savings. Years earlier, thinking of becoming a school teacher, I had been denied a government grant. Later, after I had created the leading homegrown financial services firm in Gibraltar, I happened to be sitting next to the chairman of the board of the governmental granting agency on a flight home from London.

As we were chatting, I told the gentleman that I owed him a huge thank-you. Of course, he had no idea what I was talking about. I explained to him that years earlier his board had denied me a grant to study at university.

"If I had received that grant," I explained to him, "my life would have turned out completely differently. As you know, I am doing very well and am extremely happy with my success in business."

He was not amused and sulked for the rest of the flight.

Sometimes it can give us a lot of pleasure to say our piece, albeit in an elegant and gentlemanly manner. It is a way of standing up for ourselves. Never keep things inside, because they will become toxic. Offload whatever is bothering you when the time is right. Doing so will be transformational.

THE DECISIVE MOMENT

My story is not unique. I came to a point in my life where I wanted to be free and live in my dream and not in someone else's dream. I believed in my freedom and decided not to back down from pursuing what I wanted. I persevered and didn't give up on myself, and neither must you.

Every one of us can reinvent our lives. Winning in life does not always mean you start from a position of strength. Of course, it is great whenever anyone succeeds, whether they started from a position of strength or not, but real achievement, I believe, is to be successful when you have come from behind. To be able to break through limiting beliefs and overcome a mindset that holds you back is an achievement in its own right.

A few years ago, my youngest daughter went through a challenging time at school. She was concerned about lagging behind in her assignments. I showed her a video of an athlete who, while running an important race, tripped and fell flat on her face. Another person might have given up but not that young woman. She got up, dusted herself off and, despite trailing the rest of the pack, ran like her life depended on it. She won the race. I looked at my daughter and tears were streaming down her face. She got up, said nothing, and by the end of the academic year was up-to-date with her work. She passed her exams with flying colours. We were so proud of her.

Many of us who are unable to make peace with changes that have happened in our lives go through an identity crisis. It is as if we remain stuck in the past, even though our life circumstances have changed. We don't let go, and we live in our heads—in a world that is not real or true. A false world of perceptions and emotions takes away our peace and happiness.

I believe that change can happen in an instant, while transition can take longer. Patience and perseverance are key when you are in transition.

Once, I was travelling from Israel to London, and the plane's video system broke down in the cabin in which I was sitting. I was unable to sleep and took a walk through the plane. I happened to notice a pair of earphones lying on the magazine rack. I took them and went looking for an empty seat in another cabin, hoping to watch a film.

As I walked down the aisle in the next cabin, I saw a pretty girl in the middle seat. There was an empty seat behind her, so I took it. After we landed, I tried to catch up with the girl to start a conversation. However, an elderly lady was trying to retrieve her bag from the overhead bin and blocked my way. By the time I managed to reach the terminal, the pretty girl was gone.

As I picked up my suitcase from the baggage carousel, I suddenly saw the girl and her friend about to walk through the custom's gate. I dropped my suitcase and ran after her.

"If you and I don't exchange telephone numbers," I said to her, "I will never see you again, and that would be a terrible thing."

She looked me up and down for a moment and then opened her purse to give me a business card. The rest is history, as they say. Today, that pretty girl is the mother of my three children. We have been married for over thirty years.

Transformation can happen in a moment, in the way meeting Maxine transformed my life. You have to find the courage to make a decision when it presents itself, even if your unconscious mind wants you to shy away from it. That decision will be the channel to your future.

A TRANSFORMATIONAL TOOL FOR RESOLVING CONFLICT

One of the major obstacles that keeps us from progressing in our lives is conflict. When we see a conflict from another person's point of view, we have a better understanding of the situation. Carrying the weight of discord around our necks is heavy and unforgiving and consumes our energy. When conflict is resolved, our minds and energy are free.

The first step is to imagine that you are standing in front of the person with whom you have a conflict and ask yourself the following questions:

- How am I behaving?
- How am I feeling?
- What are my beliefs about this situation?
- What is there for me to learn?

Once you have answered these questions, the second step is to visualize in your mind's eye the person standing in front of you. Then imagine you are flying out from your head and into the other person and looking at yourself through their eyes, as if you had become that person. As you do, ask the questions again: How am I behaving? How am I feeling? What are my beliefs about this situation? What is there for me to learn?

Once you are done and have, ideally, seen the situation from a different perspective, move to the next stage of the exercise.

The third step is to imagine that you fly back out of the person's head and become a fly on the wall, minding your own business and not giving two hoots about the conflict. As you look at the situation from the fly's eyes, how do you interpret it? Again, ask the four questions: How am I behaving? How am I feeling? What are my beliefs about this situation? What is there for me to learn?

When you are done, come back into your body and experience the benefit of having a deeper and wider perspective on the conflict.

This exercise will help you free yourself of attachment to the conflict. It will help you generate empathy and have a bigger point of view on the matter. Left unresolved, conflicts can blind us to opportunities because our energy is caught up in obsessively thinking about the problem we are having.

Remember, everyone has a different model of the world and experiences life through a unique set of filters and best intentions.

LET GO AND MOVE ON

When I was studying for my Master's in Creative Leadership through the school of psychotherapy and psychology at university, we discussed that a leader needs to be able to lead himself or herself before being able to lead others. We were taught the Socratic dialogue and asked to identify a conflict that we were obsessing over. I am going to share this exercise with you. I believe it will help you to let go and move on.

Sometimes, we hold on to concerns about decisions we have made. A voice in our head plagues us with doubt and accuses us of having made the wrong decision. When this happens, our thinking becomes obsessive, largely due to the unstructured nature of the arguments we formulate in our mind. The Socratic dialogue gives us the opportunity to form our thoughts into a coherent narrative, which, in turn, provides the basis for analysis, decisiveness, and closure.

Begin the exercise by identifying a situation in your life that is causing internal conflict and pulling you in two different directions. (When I did the exercise, I named the two voices in my head Kenneth and Kenny.) Write down everything that comes into your head from the point of view of both sides. Let both sides, or voices, have an honest conversation in which nothing is left unsaid.

After the dialogue is complete, try to find a reconciliation between the two sides. At the least, they can agree to disagree and no longer live in conflict with one another.

When I did the exercise, both sides expressed everything without limitation, and each voice felt vindicated. I was able to reconcile the emotional and practical implications of my experience and move on.

A Socratic dialogue can be therapeutic. It uncovers competing voices in our head and reveals our unexpressed emotions.

LOVING YOURSELF

We don't learn to love ourselves when we grow up. We are taught to criticize ourselves, at times harshly, and be our own judge, jury, and executioner. I believe that is why we unconsciously tend not to look after ourselves as adults. Self-love counters our inner critic and helps us build a healthy relationship with ourselves.

We need to include ourselves in the circle of people we love and appreciate. It sounds like a simple thing to do, but unless we make a regular practice of loving ourselves, we end up taking ourselves for granted. To make sure you don't take yourself for granted, extend love and kindness to yourself every day. Remember, you will be with yourself for the rest of your life.

Imagine a small child having to spend their life with a cruel and mentally abusive parent who judges them harshly and never thinks of them as worthy. Wouldn't you want to hug that child and give it all the love and care you could? Wouldn't you want to tell the child that they are wonderful, beautiful, and worthy of only good? That is the child that is inside of you. We all have a child inside of us who needs a loving relationship with the adult in us.

Transform your life, find yourself, and have fun! There is no need to be lonely in life when you can enjoy being with yourself.

THE POWER OF A SMILE

Transformation is available to all of us, all the time. One of the best stories of transformation that I know is about a man who was walking home from work one day. His life circumstances were so difficult that he was in deep despair and had planned to commit suicide that afternoon.

As the man was about to cross the street, a woman stopped her car to let him pass and gave him a warm smile. That smile gave him hope at a dire moment and kept him from taking his life.

Our ability to impact others in a positive way is far greater than we think. We never know how we can transform another person's life with a simple smile, and it costs us nothing.

DO YOUR BEST AND DETACH FROM THE OUTCOME

I have always had the practice of doing my best and detaching from the outcome. We can never control how anything in life is going to turn out, but we can always do our absolute best.

Ultimately, everything that happens in our lives comes from the inside. I believe that we are the creators of our universe. When I change my attitude, everything else in my life changes too. My life is a reflection of what is going on inside of me.

CONTEMPLATIONS: QUESTIONS TO ASK YOURSELF

Answer these questions and work on transforming your life:

1. How are things working in my life now and how could they be better?

2. What can I do differently to make my life better?

3. How do I decide what is right for me?

4. What bridges do I have to cross and burn behind me?

5. Three years from now, looking back on my life, what would I like to have accomplished personally and professionally?

6. What challenges do I need to face?

7. What skills do I need to acquire or improve?

8. What opportunities do I need to seek?

9. When was the last time I was grateful for everything that I have in my life?

10. What am I ready to let go of that no longer supports me?

11. What is the one most important thing I have to change or transform in my life, my career, or my business?

12. What is so worth accomplishing that I would let go of who I've been in order to become who I really am?

13. Am I allowing my life to become stagnant and, if so, what action am I going to take today in order to reconnect with my personal power and be in a state of flow?

PART THREE

HOW WILL YOU GET THERE?

CHAPTER FIVE

This Could Save Your Life

CREATE HAPPINESS THROUGH HEALTH AND FITNESS

> *Health and fitness is your pathway to an extraordinary life.*
> —KENNETH CASTIEL

In sixteen weeks' time, would you like to buy a wardrobe full of exciting new clothes, two sizes smaller than what you wear now? I did that; and if I did it, I know you can.

When I changed my lifestyle, my weight dropped by thirty pounds over a period of four months; or, as I prefer to describe it, I lost the equivalent of thirty, one-pound bags of sugar that I had been hauling around for years.

How did I lose all that weight and build strength and fitness? Did I have a magic wand? In one sense, I did, because I reduced my waist from a dangerous thirty-seven inches (I was beginning to look like I was pregnant!) to a good-looking, healthy thirty-two inches. My back pain, which had been crippling me around the clock for more than twenty years and prevented me from helping my wife carry shopping bags at the supermarket, disappeared and never returned.

Not only did I stop snoring, I stopped my sleep apnoea. I used to go to bed at night and never feel fully rested in the morning. Often, I felt more tired in the morning than when I went to bed the night before. My wife no longer wakes up in a panic in the middle of the night, thinking I am about to die because I stopped breathing for a few seconds between snores. Sometimes, I stopped breathing for so long that she nearly had a heart attack.

How many one-pound bags of sugar are you hauling around in extra weight? What kind of impact is it having on your health and relationships? What kind of impact will it have on your life five, ten, or fifteen years from now?

Imagine the Starship Enterprise from the Star Trek television series leaking oil or being mechanically unfit when under attack from an enemy Klingon vessel that wants to blow it to smithereens.

Visualize your body as the Starship Enterprise and realise that, sooner or later, you will be under attack from either a disease or an accident—everyone eventually is. The stronger and fitter we are, the greater are the chances that we will pull through and make a full recovery.

THE VALUE OF CHANGING YOUR LIFESTYLE

I had been on medication for high blood pressure and cholesterol for years. After I lost weight, the doctor monitored me for a while and then advised me to stop taking most of those medicines because I no longer needed them. No doctor had ever told me that if I changed my lifestyle and lost weight, I would be able to reduce my medications or stop taking them altogether.

I remember the day when I was first prescribed the medications. The doctor told me that I would be taking them for the rest of my life. It was as if he was giving me a life sentence.

Prescribing medication, which is necessary in some cases, tends to become a quick fix. Doctors have limited time in their busy schedules, and people prioritize other things in life over their health. People repeat the programming they have inherited from their parents. If a parent took pills every day, chances are so will the next generation. The pharmaceutical companies, whose future profits depend on people taking medications rather than adopting a healthy lifestyle, are also to blame. I sometimes think they are in conspiracy with the food and sugar industry. Haven't we all been enticed by chocolates, sweets, and biscuits when we queue up to pay for petrol or stand in line at the grocery checkout? For anyone attempting to maintain healthy eating and lifestyle choices, these easy-access temptations make it incredibly challenging unless you live with purpose, which means you make the decision to keep away from what doesn't serve you before you ever come in contact with it.

On my main street, they opened a shop which sells exotic chocolates. For the first few weeks after it had opened, I walked on the other side of the road every single day to consciously avoid the temptation. After a few weeks of ignoring it, I could walk past it and not even notice it was there. Through repetition I trained my unconscious mind to just block it out. The villain within will use every trick in the book to tempt you. You just have to be strong and wise, and instead, embrace the hero within you so you win at the game of life.

The motivation to change my lifestyle and pursue a life of health and fitness did not originate in health issues. My big "why" for taking action arose when I saw my father pass away at the age of eighty-nine.

Many people may claim that eighty-nine is a ripe old age. Our perception of life expectancy can make that seem true, but the quality of my dear father's life due to ill health had not been good for many years. He'd been in and out of the hospital since the age of sixty-five, when he had quadruple bypass heart surgery and nearly didn't survive.

My father depended exclusively on medication and, like many people, didn't take responsibility for his health and fitness. He thought taking pills was the panacea to his health issues, but, obviously, that wasn't true. I don't remember my father ever saying he had to lose weight and get fit because the doctor told him to or that he'd read it was a good thing to do.

In the past, perhaps, people were less aware. There weren't gymnasiums everywhere like there are today. Cigarettes were advertised on television, and consumers were encouraged to smoke. The world was excited by the new drugs which kept diabetes, high blood pressure, and cholesterol at bay. People didn't think about the long-term side effects of drugs on their kidneys and other vital organs.

My father had a big sweet tooth and, though he was diabetic, he consumed desserts full of sugar. He relied on the false security that he would be fine if he took his medicine. Instead, he injured his heart and other organs for years.

Eventually, his kidneys stopped working, and he ended up on dialysis.

I remember seeing my father depend on others to care for him around the clock. My wonderful mother dedicated her life to looking after him. His muscles wasted away because he hadn't built up his strength when he was younger. It got to the point that he didn't have the strength to get out of bed or out of a chair without assistance.

My father used to tell me to look after my health, but it didn't dawn on me until some years later to do so. He knew what it was like to live with deteriorating health. He tried to fight his illnesses, but he didn't have any weapons to defend himself against them. He hadn't taken action to build his strength and remain fit and healthy when he had the time. He wasn't ready for a battle with a formidable enemy—an army led by old age and the ravages of thirty-five years of diabetes, hypertension, kidney dysfunction, and the double-edged sword of daily pills. Sadly, he fought with his hands tied behind his back and his ankles shackled. My father is an example of a situation in which many people find themselves today.

If a huge army were on its way to destroy you, would you look the other way for thirty years and live in denial, thinking the army will never arrive? When it finally does, you won't be prepared or have weapons to defend yourself with. You will be at the mercy of an overwhelming enemy. The cruel enemy doesn't want to kill you, only to torture you for as long as it can keep you alive. It starts by taking away your dignity.

If you were aware that your beloved child was going to be captured and tortured in thirty years, wouldn't you do everything in your power to protect him or her?

When I saw my father pass away, I recalled that, though he had lived to the age of eighty-nine, he had spent fifteen years fighting a cruel army that took away the quality and enjoyment of his life. We are all going to die. I'm confident none of us will escape it. But why would anyone want to sow the seeds of unnecessary suffering? Why choose to spend the last ten to fifteen years of your life fighting with your hands tied behind your back, when you could adopt a healthy lifestyle today, build your strength, and enjoy a good quality of life for as long as possible?

What I am asking you to do doesn't come with a cast-iron guarantee, but it does give you a splendid opportunity to live life on your own terms. Most importantly, take action now so that you don't have to give up your dignity and independence years before you have to pack up your bags and leave this earth forever!

GO BEYOND WHERE YOU ARE NOW

My wife Maxine and I set goals to remain fit and healthy and to continue travelling as we become older. We want to embark on new adventures, discover new horizons, go to the gym every day, make love, be involved in business and charitable projects, help our children build their empires, take our grandchildren on exciting experiences, and do all of this and more well into our eighties, nineties, and hundreds.

Is that too ambitious? I don't think so. When you truly want something, you invest time and energy into acquiring it. You don't have to follow the status quo and society's programming. You must adopt a whatever-it-takes attitude instead. Change agreements that say you can't do something to robust ones that say you can. Become bulletproof, be proactive, and stay in charge of creating a fit and healthy lifestyle.

When I walk down the street, I sadly see that not much has changed in the last thirty to forty years. There may be a gym in every neighbourhood, but the challenge to stay fit is not going away. We still have an obesity epidemic.

"According to estimates from Public Health England, two-thirds of adults and a quarter of children between two and ten years old are overweight or obese. Obese children are more likely to become overweight adults and to suffer premature ill health and mortality, and by 2034, seventy per cent of adults are expected to be overweight or obese."* Statistics in other European countries and the United States are no better, or even worse.

Obesity increases the risk of a number of health issues, including heart disease, stroke, diabetes, musculoskeletal disorders, cancers, depression, and anxiety.

The day Maxine and I went out to buy me a new wardrobe of clothes became a major milestone in my life. It wasn't only about buying new clothes. It represented my ability to tap into my personal power, rewrite the details of my destiny, and reaffirm to myself that I could turn around a major situation in my life. I was like a child who had been let loose in a toy shop. I had so much fun buying new clothes. It made me realise, once again, that we can achieve anything we put our minds to.

All my old clothes that were too big for me went to the charity shop. I know some people keep their old clothes in case they gain weight, and guess what? Their unconscious minds make good on the expectation and, within a year or two, their old clothes fit perfectly again. They created a self-fulfilling prophecy. The unconscious mind always

---

* Davies, D. and Bhatia, T. (2015). "Can the NHS help tackle the UK's obesity epidemic?" Nuffield Trust Blog. 2015. Available at: https://www.nuffieldtrust.org.uk/news-item/can-the-nhs-help-tackle-the-uk-s-obesity-epidemic.

acts as if your wish is its command. So be careful what you wish for, whether verbally or nonverbally, because the unconscious mind always delivers.

I believe we have been created to prove to ourselves that we can go beyond wherever we may be at a given moment. Doing so makes us confident individuals. If you deliver on the promises that you make to yourself time and again, your self-esteem will go through the roof and your confidence will break the glass ceiling.

TAKE THE FIRST STEP AND MAKE IT FUN!

Take your first step now—not next week, next month, or when your friend can join you. Honour the beautiful, wonderful self that you are and invest in the magical vehicle that is your body.

Our bodies want to serve us if we allow it. Ever since you were a cute baby in your mother's arms, your body has wanted to carry you on exciting new journeys to wonderful places—a gift that I am grateful for every day of my life.

Perhaps you are in the middle of a situation in your life that is preventing you from becoming aware of the gift of your body. Maybe you don't believe that it is never too late to create health, strength, and fitness. I appreciate that it might be hard to begin with, but remember, a voyage of a thousand leagues starts with a single step. It is as simple as that! Just take one step at a time and set simple weekly goals.

I know we all have stories that hold us back. I, too, have had them, but I learnt over many years that we are powerful beyond measure and deserving of everything good. If you disagree, I recommend you speak with a professional who can help you. If, for whatever reason, any of us believes we are not worthy, the thought will roam our psyches and impede our progress. It will sabotage everything we do. So, please seek advice if this applies to you. It is easier than you may think.

Get up extra early tomorrow morning and go for a walk. Take that first step! Use the power of music to inspire and carry you. Let all the muscles in your face break into a beautiful smile while you look at life through soft eyes, knowing that everything is fine in the here and now.

Don't just read these words. Please, act on them! I love you, and I want you to succeed.

TRUST THAT YOUR LIFE CAN BE BETTER

There are times in life when we must take things on faith, and you may be experiencing one of those times. Remember that the airlines say to put your mask on first before you help your fellow passengers. If you don't look after yourself, you won't be able to care for anyone else.

Take the cute baby who lives within you and look after it. If anyone—friends, family, or coworker—is cynical about your journey and the new and exciting expectations you have for yourself, know that they are cynical because they have not yet found the self-motivation and courage to change their own lives. No one likes to fail on their own, so, by stopping you, they are assured of company. Send them to me at facebook.com/kennethcastiel, and I will speak to them, but don't let them turn you around. You are standing on the threshold, taking a momentous and decisive step toward the rest of your life.

The decisions we make transform our life journey. They lead us to people, opportunities, and possibilities. When we get out of our head and wake up in the here and now, we discover that everything is in a state of becoming. We must all take that critical first step, or the force of habit will create resistance.

You may have no idea what is possible for you. Nothing in your wildest dreams could prepare you for the good that awaits you once you take the first step.

The universe doesn't want to give us charity. I believe we are loved too much to be given charity. We need to work hard so we can feel good about ourselves when we achieve our goals. No parent wants to give its child handouts, because doing so would undermine their child's potential. This life is a journey of discovery of what is possible, including health and physical fitness, so that we can maximize our life.

The train to a better and healthier life is moving out of the station. Do you have the courage to jump aboard and leave behind everything that doesn't serve you? Once the train gathers speed, it will be difficult to catch up, and there may not be another train coming by soon. So, put on your trainers—if you don't own a pair, wear any shoes—and just jump on the train! You will never look back once you do.

ENJOY ACTIVITY

Physical fitness does not have to be a lonely, monotonous, or boring activity. Taking the first step could mean joining a gym or going for a jog or brisk walk with a friend. It could be joining a dance group. I have friends who joined a dance club, and they have had so much fun. It has become the social event of their week. Maxine and I became members of a tennis club and have amazing fun playing paddle tennis. When we are using the subway in London, we climb the escalators instead of standing still and having the escalators carry us.

Table tennis is also a great exercise. Taking the stairs instead of the lift creates momentum. Not using the car when you visit a friend who lives around the corner or when going to the neighbourhood shops and cafes will transform a sedentary lifestyle into one of motion.

The challenge is not the activity itself nor the time it takes to do it. The challenge is to make the commitment and execute the plan. The way forward is through committing and taking massive action.

If you have been inactive for a long time, be sure to get your doctor's advice before you embark on an exercise programme. Call your doctor now and make an appointment. Don't leave it till next week. Listen to the hero within you, harness the force, and be sure your inner dialogue motivates you and keeps you upbeat.

Whatever you do has to be consistent. Action taken regularly will get results. Your family and friends will notice that you are different. Within only a few weeks, they may see a physical change.

I used to have a visceral fat count of fifteen; now, it is ten. Visceral fat wraps around our vital organs. I didn't know what visceral fat was until I started working with a personal trainer. My body fat dropped from 30 to 19 percent. My body age went from sixty-one to thirty-two.

I had no idea that was possible until I started training with a professional. (At the time, I joked with my twenty-eight-year-old son that I was only four years older than him).

The longer you wait to get physically fit, the harder your climb will be. If you are forty when you begin, it will be tougher than if you had started when you were thirty-five. Likewise, if you are sixty, it will be much easier than waiting until you are seventy or seventy-five to begin exercising. Whatever age you are, start now as it is never too late!

GET EXPERT ADVICE

The first step I took was to hire a personal trainer. I did not want to become a person who went to the gym every day and never shed a pound. I believe it is important to get expert advice. We do it all the time when it comes to our legal, medical, and financial matters. Why not the same for fitness and nutrition? Some personal trainers are knowledgeable in both.

I recommend interviewing several trainers before selecting one to work with. Do your due diligence and make sure you are comfortable with the person you choose. Feel free to ask questions about the results they have achieved with other people like you and inquire if you can speak with current or former clients.

Resist the voice inside your head that says you can't afford a trainer. Nothing could be as important as your health, fitness, and strength. Delay buying the next smartphone for a few months and invest in the future of your health instead. You may not need a trainer for the rest of your life. It may only be necessary for a few months.

One of the most valuable benefits of having a personal trainer is that he or she will keep you accountable, and accountability will have enormous power in your success. I see my personal trainer three times a week and enjoy the sessions. It is better to delegate what you need to do to a professional rather than trying to work it out on your own. My personal trainer gave me sound nutritional advice and helped me achieve amazing results.

CHANGE THE SCHOOL CURRICULUM

We learn many fine things at school—math, English, science—but there are other important subjects that aren't taught in schools: how to look after ourselves, how to create a good lifestyle, and how to eat in a healthy way.

A few years ago, the British parliament debated the impact of sugar on health and the rise in diabetes that was expected in coming years due to its presence in consumable products such as fizzy drinks, chocolates, and sweets. I was so impressed that I called a local school and encouraged them to introduce the topic to children in the school. She declined, saying there wasn't enough time in the school day to add a discussion of the harmful effects of sugar into the curriculum.

I was shocked that she wasn't interested in teaching youngsters how to be healthy, strong individuals. Doing so would be a lot cheaper than treating their ailments later in life. School curricula could be an ideal way to change the conditioning of the next generation.

DIETS DON'T WORK

Unfortunately, diets don't work and end up creating a yo-yo effect. We get caught in a cycle of putting on weight and losing it, then putting weight back on again and going on another diet. I know people who have been on hundreds of diets, and they still struggle with their weight.

The only way to make a lasting change in our weight is through changing our lifestyle. A change of lifestyle is empowering and makes us feel like a new person. Change begins in the mind when we question our conditioned ideas. The reasons for being overweight lie in the mind.

THROW OUT THE COOKIES

Once you have made the decision to get fit, rid your

kitchen of food that gets in the way of your progress. Throw everything that isn't good for you into the rubbish, even if you hate wasting the money. Maxine and I did the chore together, empowering and helping each other. We cleared out all the food that didn't serve us at the time, including sugar, cookies, cheese, alcohol, pasta, potatoes, and bread. If you live with other people and can't throw everything away, dedicate one cupboard for your food and another for everyone else's food.

I embarked on a twelve-week diet, and during that time I made sure I was never within an arm's length of any temptations during meal time. On the advice of my personal trainer, I drank between eight to ten glasses of water a day (and more during the summer). My life, as I have said, dramatically changed for the better, and I want nothing less than the same for you. What is a few weeks of overcoming challenges in the context of a great lifetime?

Unfortunately, many people do not realise that losing weight alone will not change their bodies. You must also build muscle, which begins to waste away as we age. When muscles waste, we have difficulty with balance and walking. We need to change our lifestyle *and* get fit to be strong enough to do the simplest things, such as get out of a chair on our own when we're older, not simply to look good. Remember, we are preparing to fight an army led by old age and potential disease. That is why we need help from professionals.

The scales don't tell the whole story about physical health. When we become fit, we build muscle, and muscle carries weight. Do not get discouraged if your weight doesn't drop as much as you would like, and don't become attached to weighing a certain number. The key is to transform fat into lean muscle. A good personal trainer will know how to help you and will teach you stretching exercises to help get rid of everyday aches and pains, which most people believe are chronic.

A good friend of mine from England was so surprised when he saw how I had transformed physically that he was inspired to change his eating habits and get fit, too. He gave up bread, pasta, sugar, and potatoes for twelve weeks, and each day he went for a one-and-a-half-hour power walk with his partner, even during the rain and snow. He shed twelve kilos (twenty-six pounds) because he was committed and consistent.

Don't feel guilty if you indulge now and then or give in to a temptation. One pizza will not destroy your health. Simply pick yourself up, dust yourself off and carry on with your healthy lifestyle. Too many people give up simply because they tripped up once. Don't be one of them. Just succeed as many times as you fail, plus one.

IT IS NEVER TOO LATE

I have emphasized elsewhere in this book the importance of commitment, so ask yourself if you are willing to work hard for your physical well-being. Visualize yourself ten or fifteen years into the future, assuming you continue on the same path. What would it feel and look like to live in your body then?

Define your goals and be sure to share them with your personal trainer. How many kilograms (pounds) do you wish to lose in the weeks ahead? If you do not want to lose weight, share that with your trainer, too. Let your desire for how you want to look and feel in the future pull you in the direction of change.

Some people believe they are too unhealthy or overweight to change and that nothing they do could make a difference. I know from experience that there is no such thing as a point of no return.

You are here on this beautiful planet, so why not use the time you have to honour yourself by getting fit and healthy? When you do, you can look forward to enjoying many wonderful, healthy years.

I always get a lump in my throat when I read this poem by Walter D. Wintle. I imagine the author is talking directly to me. It became my self-fulfilling prophecy.

If you think you are beaten, you are;
If you think you dare not, you don't.
If you'd like to win, but you think you can't,
It is almost a certain—you won't.

If you think you'll lose, you've lost;
For out in this world we find
Success begins with a fellow's will
It's all in the state of mind.

If you think you're outclassed, you are;
You've got to think high to rise.
You've got to be sure of yourself before
You can ever win the prize.

Life's battles don't always go
To the stronger or faster man;
But sooner or later the man who wins
Is the one who thinks he can!

CONTEMPLATIONS: QUESTIONS TO ASK YOURSELF

The questions below will help you highlight the importance of living a healthy lifestyle. Contemplate the questions below thoroughly and write down your responses.

A. HEALTHY LIFESTYLE

1. If you don't now enjoy a healthy lifestyle, why do you think that is?

For me, not exercising and eating unhealthily became a habit.

2. What is it that you are prepared to do to adopt a healthy lifestyle?

- For me, it was throwing out any food that didn't serve me, at least in the short term while I was losing weight. These were: potatoes, pasta, deserts, bread, sugar, and chocolates. I hardly drink any alcohol, but if you do, that one also counts.
- I consulted a nutritionist, set healthy lifestyle goals, and aligned the way I ate with my new goals.
- I also employed an amazing personal trainer and started training three times a week. She kept me accountable, safe from injuries, and my weight started falling off. I adopted a healthy lifestyle instead of going on a diet, and the weight has never returned.
- I was coachable and followed what the experts said.

3. Make a list of what you are going to need for becoming fit and healthy.

For example, you may already have a pair of trainers, but not a personal trainer to guide you.

4. How will you be able to confirm that you have reached your goal when you do?

For me, it was being able to wear a thirty-two-waist trouser.

5. What will a fit and healthy lifestyle do for you and permit you to do?

It raised my self-esteem, gave me peace of mind, and allowed me to be involved in sporting activities such as cycling, sprinting, and mountain trekking. I love these activities and have so much fun doing them with my children.

6. Are you prepared to take massive action and full responsibility for achieving your results?

If my wife hadn't wanted to become fit and healthy and share the same goal, I would have done it on my own. Nothing between heaven and earth would have stopped me from getting my result.

7. When you arrive at your goal, what will your life look like with regard to people, places, timelines, and your ability to plan for a positive and motivating future?

Use the visualization exercise for creating your future to create an image of you with a healthy lifestyle. You will find this exercise just before the contemplations at the end of Chapter 3. Imagine that the image has a remote control with dials that control volume, colour, brightness, and contrast. Use the imaginary remote control to make the image as strong and vivid as possible. Now (this is the fun part!), imagine that you are flying out of your head and into the future. Trust yourself and drop the image into the future, making sure you see yourself in the image.

8. I knew this could be achieved, as I have seen other people succeed at becoming fit and healthy. Do you know anybody who has? Guess what, you know me, and if I could do it, so can you.

9. So, let's summarize and find your purpose for enjoying a life of health and fitness. Please answer these questions:

- **Why do you want to be fit and healthy?**
    - I want to enjoy an outstanding quality of life as I get older.
- **What will take place in your life when you are fit and healthy?**
    - Friends started stopping me in the street and complimenting me on how well and young I looked.

Every time this happens, I feel successful and empowered.
- **What will not manifest in your life when you are fit and healthy?**
  - For me, it was not having to make medication a way of living.
- **If you don't get fit and healthy, what will be missing in your life?**
  - For me, it was good mobility and no back pain. I know that if I hadn't gotten fit and healthy, I would have ended up having a very serious back operation.*

B. FOOD

1. What is my relationship with food?
2. Do I eat for comfort? If so, what pain am I trying to comfort?
3. What do I need to give up that no longer serves me?
4. What would happen to my health if I changed my relationship with food?

C. MINDFUL EATING

1. Am I fully present when I eat, or am I in my head thinking about something else?
2. Am I mindful of every bite I take?

---
* Inspired by the work of Tad James.

3. Do I enjoy chewing and tasting my food?
4. Am I aware when I swallow my food?

D. RITUAL EATING

1. Do I eat when I am hungry?
2. Do I eat when I am not hungry?
3. Do I eat according to the time of the day?
4. Do I chew my food properly, especially when I am eating meat?
5. Do I have a ritual for having a dessert or something sweet after a meal?

CHAPTER SIX

What Is Your Excuse?

LET'S CREATE MORE TIME IN YOUR LIFE

Whatever you can do, or dream you can, begin it. Boldness has genius, power, and magic in it.
—GOETHE

A lack of time is one of the most common excuses people use for not making changes in their lives. I, too, procrastinated before writing this book. Once I committed, however, I found the time and realised that my procrastination was due to a fear of both succeeding and failing. My unconscious mind tried to protect me from the hard work necessary to turn an idea into reality.

On one hand, I was excited about sharing my ideas with the world, while on the other, I was apprehensive about the loneliness I might experience spending so much time writing. Also, I knew that a book was the tip of the iceberg of a big business venture at a time in life when most of my contemporaries were contemplating retirement. I would have to invest time and money and take risks. Lastly, I did not want to taint my track record of success in business if I failed.

One of my mentors taught me, as I was starting in business many years ago, that failure is never an option. You only fail when you complain, make excuses, and do nothing. If I hadn't taken massive action and pushed the pendulum to the opposite side—to where I resisted going—you would not be reading this book and many people would not be participating in my programmes.

In many ways, we craft our destiny by how we respond to the opportunities and challenges life presents us with. It does not matter what our age is or where we are in our lives. My mother spends four hours three times a week connected to a dialysis machine. She drives herself to and from the hospital and motivates the other patients while she's there. She is upbeat about her life, never complains, and has a smile and a good word for everyone. She is an inspiration.

When we stop procrastinating, we begin moving with

the natural rhythm of life. You will never find a tree, a flower, or nature being grumpy or procrastinating about who they were born to be. When you move, the universe moves with you and helps you steer events in your life. If we do not move, how can the universe steer? Have you ever tried steering a car with the handbrake on?

In life, we end up with results or excuses. I like results, so I don't allow excuses to enter my life, no matter how long it takes me or what I need to do to achieve what I set out to do.

Some years ago, my eldest daughter applied to university. The system allowed her to apply to five universities. She was accepted by four out of the five. The school she wanted to attend the most, and that offered the degree she was passionate about, rejected her. Did she give up? Not at all. She accepted the situation and developed a strategy. She attended one of the universities that had accepted her, worked hard, and got a top grade at the end of her first year. She reapplied to the university that rejected her and was one of thirty students who were accepted out of the three hundred who had applied.

I love that attitude of never giving up and continuing the fight, even when it could be reasonable to accept a negative outcome. As motivational speaker Les Brown says, "It's not over until I win." When you believe and internalise his words, you will see results. Make the decision now!

BE THE OBSERVER OF YOUR LIFE

I once had a salesperson who came to me at the end of each month to report that she had not sold anything. When I asked her if she had spoken to and prospected at least five people each working day of the month—the benchmark for success in sales—she replied that she had not. She gave herself excuses instead, not results.

When baking a fruitcake, you must follow the recipe. If you follow the recipe for chocolate cake you won't end up with fruitcake. The strategies I am giving you are tried and tested. If you follow the methodology like you would a recipe, you will be fine.

Remember to be the observer of your life. The villain inside you will always make you doubt that you can succeed.

The villain does not like uncertainty or the unknown and will use it to frighten you. If we don't want fear to control our lives, we have to let it go and take refuge in the here and now where everything is fine most of the time.

Fear—unless you are in danger, in which case you must run away—is a figment of your imagination, as I have explained in this book. We create a scary film and watch it time and again on the screen of your mind.

I ask my clients what would happen to their worries and their fears if they died tomorrow.

Sometimes we need shock treatment to wake up from the nearly hypnotic state we get ourselves into. My mother says, "If you worry, you die, and if you don't worry, you also die. So why worry?"

Always be aware that making a decision is a form of transportation, comparable to taking a train. A decision transports you to a destination in the same way a train does. Decisions, and the boldness to make them, are conduits to places, people, and results. Without decisions, you are stuck and fear rules. If we insist on having to know exactly what is on the other side of a doorway that leads to the future, we will never be able to find the courage to cross the threshold.

> "Come to the edge," he said.
> "We can't. We're afraid!" they responded.
> "Come to the edge," he said.
> "We can't. We will fall!" they responded.
> "Come to the edge," he said.
> And so they came.
> And he pushed them.
> And they flew.
>
> —GUILLAUME APOLLINAIRE

I especially like the story of the prisoner who faced

imminent death to illustrate the immeasurable value of confronting our fears, and how we have much to lose when we don't:

A prisoner of war faced a death sentence. Shortly before his execution, the captain of the contingent escorted the prisoner from his cell. He took the man to a door and had him stand in front of it. He gave the prisoner a choice. Tomorrow morning at dawn, he explained, he could either go through the door or face a firing squad.

The prisoner asked the captain what lay on the other side of the door. The captain replied that he was unable to provide any further details. Anything could lie on the other side of the door. He could only give the prisoner the opportunity to walk through the doorway and find out for himself, or face certain death if he chose the firing squad.

The prisoner returned to his cell, and the following morning was brought back to the captain.

"Have you made your choice?" the captain asked.

"I choose the firing squad," the prisoner replied.

Within a few minutes, the sound of shots rang out. Inside the captain's office, the captain's secretary asked what was on the other side of the door.

"Freedom," he answered, "but most people are too scared of the unknown to choose it."

The story captures the essence of what we do too often. We allow our mind to invent the worst possible scenario about the future, and then we refuse to walk through the doorway into the unknown.

Though we normally do not have to face anything as absolute as a firing squad, we do accept situations that don't serve us well or could harm us in order to avoid the unknown. What we don't realise is that life will keep presenting us with unknown adventures for as long as we are alive. It is the only way we grow. When we hide and do not dance with life, we fall into depression and suffer anxiety. We are pulled in two directions—the hero wants us to win and the villain wants us to fail.

I had a client who was miserable in her job for years. She was paid less than her male peers, even though she worked as hard as they did. The atmosphere in the office where she worked was tense and unfriendly, but she was scared of the unknown and would not change jobs. I worked with her on breaking through her fear. She now loves her new job and says she wishes she had made the move ten years earlier.

The tools in this book will help you break the boundaries

that hold you back and enable you to reach new heights in your life.

> Mortality is a big motivator to change.
>
> Most of us think we will live forever. None of us wants to confront death, but when a doctor tells us that we have three months to live, we suddenly look at our lives differently. We no longer tolerate behaviour that we once accepted. We throw away our clothes and start dressing the way we have always wanted, regardless of who may get upset.
>
> When we believe that we have a long life ahead of us, we tend to comply with others' expectations for us, in order to be liked, and forfeit our authenticity.
>
> Though I expect to have a long life, I live as if I only have six months left to live. If you adopt this strategy, it will give you a sense of urgency and be an antidote to sitting on your laurels. After all, how do you, or any of us, know that we don't have six months to live? Live with passion today!

TIME MANAGEMENT AND DELEGATION MATTER

Looking at our relationship with health and fitness is one way to appreciate how we hold ourselves back from making changes.

The charity Diabetes UK has warned that by the year 2025 five million people in UK will develop diabetes, which is double the number from five years ago. The vast majority of diabetes sufferers have type 2 diabetes, which is linked to obesity, poor diet, and a sedentary lifestyle. I was shocked to learn that more than seventy thousand deaths a year are due to diabetes—one in seven of all deaths.

In the United States, a recent analysis from the Center for Disease Control and Prevention states that as many as one in three adults in the United States could have diabetes by 2050 if current sky-rocketing trends continue. Even more shocking is the fact that only one in ten of them have diabetes now.

I am not a doctor and will not discuss health issues, but I cite the above information in order to shine a light on the importance of prioritizing your time so that you have a better, healthier quality of life.

You have only one life to live, and what you do with it is up to you. When you take responsibility for yourself, you win at the game of life. When you give up your power by blaming others for your circumstances, chances are that you will lose in life. Life is too precious to resign yourself to that.

I have a friend who is an importer from the United States. When the U.S. dollar is weak, he says his business is doing well; however, when the dollar is strong, he complains that business is bad. He depends on an external factor to determine his profitability, instead of diversifying and making smarter business decisions.

TIME MANAGEMENT

We all have twenty-four hours in a day, yet each of us achieves different results in our lives. Why is that? I believe that time is never an excuse. It's how we prioritize our time that determines whether we are successful or not in any field of endeavour.

People say that they can't go to the gym because they don't have time. I tell them that they don't go because they choose not to. They just use lack of time as an excuse. Prioritizing time means doing in your twenty-four hours the things that are important to you—and important does not necessarily include what you want to do.

I put health and fitness high on my list of priorities, next to oxygen, which doesn't mean that I'm always in the mood to train. Nonetheless, I make the commitment and simply do it. I set aside time with my trainer three times a week—ahead of work, watching television, chatting with friends, or an extra hour in bed.

Most people know that when they hire a personal trainer—even if it is only for three months—they are committing to changing their lifestyle, eating healthily, losing weight, and getting fitter within a relatively short period of time. I know it's true because I did it. Many of us, however, don't want to be held accountable or meet the demands, even though we are prepared to be accountable to our doctor when we don't look after ourselves and must take medication for the rest of our lives.

We become set in our ways, and it becomes a matter of urgency to smash through the glass ceiling of complexity. By complexity, I mean all the activities and commitments we have taken on over the years that don't add value to our lives. If you were on a ship in the middle of the ocean that was taking in water, wouldn't you throw everything overboard to give more time for the rescue services to arrive?

We have to create space in our lives so we can embark on new and worthwhile ventures. You must seriously consider throwing overboard the things in your life that are sinking your boat. If we continually take on more than we can manage, we will end up like the poor donkey travelling through the desert whose owner keeps putting one sack after another on its back. Eventually, the donkey falls flat on its face.

Socializing often occurs around food and drink, and many people who are committed to a path of health and fitness change their social circles when they decide to eat in new ways.

You may say that you have a sweet tooth. I can assure you that you don't know what a sweet tooth is until you meet me. If there is chocolate in the house, I will find it, so my solution is to not keep chocolate anywhere near me. I eat an apple instead.

If we want the kind of well-being that enables us to participate in all that life offers, we must look at the association between pain and pleasure. We need to find the courage to choose the right path instead of pursuing the familiar, easy ones like we always have.

I love the story I heard about a man driving along the highway. He stopped at a filling station and walked inside to pay for his petrol. There was a whining dog lying next to the door. He asked the assistant what was wrong with the dog. The clerk told him that the dog was lying on a nail. "Why doesn't he move?" the man asked. "Because it's not hurting him enough," the assistant replied.

Once things start to hurt too much, it may be too late. We may already have a heart attack or stroke by then. In truth, it is never too late to change. Don't let things develop to the point that you have to climb an even steeper hill to return to a healthy life.

Remember that the purpose of having good health is to enjoy life, which includes having fun with your children and grandchildren—and even great grandchildren. Let your legacy inspire the next generation to live a healthy life. Use your time wisely and prioritize!

DELEGATION

People often have difficulty managing their time because of a lack of trust. Delegating tasks requires trust in another person's ability to do the job. When we take on more responsibilities and commitments, we need confidence in others so they can help us carry the load, even if we have to pay them.

I have always recruited the right people for the job, paid generous salaries, and invested time and money into training recruits. Then, I am confident when I delegate. I believe in delegating everything except my unique skills, which only I should do. Delegating creates more energy and spaciousness in life.

Business owners who do not delegate handicap themselves and are unable to create a business model that can run without them. They maintain the boss-employee model without realising that they are as constrained as their employees.

When you run a business without being involved in every detail, you are able to scale it. I built the leading homegrown financial services firm in my country, and it became a valuable asset that I went on to sell because it didn't need me. The value of the business lies in the people and systems I developed and implemented.

An inability to delegate affects our personal relationships, which suffer when we are too busy to socialize. Countless successful people make a great deal of money, but end up without a family or getting divorced. When I coach my entrepreneurial clients, I tell them that if they implement the strategies I teach, they will be able to have it all—business success, happy family, and a healthy lifestyle. I know because I did it. I teach what I know works from my own personal experience.

I remember a story Jim Rohn used to tell. Every day, a little girl experienced her father coming home from work. He used to pat her on the head and continue working at home. The little girl was upset and told her mother that her daddy didn't love her. Her mother re-assured her and explained that her daddy loved her very much, just that he couldn't finish all the work he had in the office and had to bring it home with him. The little girl thought for a moment and said, "Why don't they put him in a slower group then?" You have to consider the garden you are sowing as one day you are going to reap what you have sowed. I can say with my hand in my hand that I have never brought home work with me.

Back problems and other ailments consistently plague the overly busy and over-committed person and have a profound effect on quality of life. What good is success in business without being successful at life? Only good health and fulfilling relationships truly make us happy.

I explain to people I coach that if they find a problem in their daily lives, it belongs to them. If they can't resolve it, they need to find someone who can, instead of ignoring it. When I walk down the street and see a discarded can of cola, I pick it up and place it in a rubbish bin, believing that it's my responsibility to keep my country tidy.

MAKE EXCUSES OR ENJOY RESULTS

Time management involves coordinating the various components of our lives based on answers to the following essential questions:

- Where am I now?
- Where do I truly want to go?
- How am I going to get there?

You need a plan, or a map of the journey. Imagine setting off by car from Los Angeles to New York without a map to guide you. When we begin our day waiting for someone to tell us what to do, we never get to where we want to go. Without a plan, our time does not belong to us; it belongs to someone else.

By planning your time in advance, you refuse to allow the monkey in your head to jump from branch to branch and take you on a tour of things not relevant to your goal. By having a plan, you bypass the turbulence of your mind.

Did you know that we have tens of thoughts a minute? The more thoughts we have, the less we can cope and the more lethargic we become. We fall into a state of overwhelm. When we have a plan, we move forward without distractions or procrastination, similar to when we were in school and had a schedule. We went from one lesson to the next until the day was complete.

Unfortunately, when we don't plan but make excuses instead, our unconscious mind is not motivated to support us. The unconscious mind knows when we are lying and doesn't like liars. How would you like to live with someone who promises to do many things and when the day comes, nothing happens? It's a form of abuse, and much of the time we do it to ourselves. We create a war inside ourselves—one part of us wants to live in integrity and another part wants to sabotage that intention. Depression can sometimes be a symptom of not living in integrity. When we don't deliver to ourselves it is highly probable that we will not like ourselves, and that can lead to anxiety and depression.

Time management requires careful consideration and implementation. In order to be effective, we must align ourselves with the part of ourselves that refuses to make excuses and wants good results—the hero within!

TECHNIQUES FOR MANAGING YOUR LIFE

Once we are aligned with the hero within—the part of us that wants to succeed and live with integrity—techniques can help us flourish.

You have to be hungry for success; if you aren't, act as if you are. Your unconscious mind doesn't know the difference and will assist you, believing you are ravenous for success in any area of life. So, get up like a lion in the morning, even if you don't feel like it, and create your plan!

One technique I have found to be useful is to spend eight hours of the day doing the things that I *want* to do, eight hours on those activities I *have to* do, and eight hours *sleeping*. By distilling my time down to these three basic components, I am able to manage my time in a balanced, motivating way.

Observe a small child whose mother tells her that if she puts her toys away, she will get chocolate ice cream. Do you think she will put her toys away? Of course, she will. It's the same with us; in fact, I believe there is a part of us that never grows up. The unconscious mind wants to have fun, too, which is why you set aside eight hours a day for the things you want to do.

At this point in your life, you may feel you have to dedicate ten hours a day to the things you have to do and only six hours to the things you want to do. I felt the same once, but I created a lifestyle which affords me however much free time I choose to have. That was my goal, and I am happy to say that I achieved it.

DO NOT OVERLOOK THE DETAILS

Never touch the same piece of paper or digital correspondence twice. Deal with every item once only, either by delegating it or taking care of it yourself. Do not keep looking at it.

If you have a magazine you want to read, put it in your briefcase. If the next month's issue arrives before you have had time to read the one in your briefcase, ditch the outdated one and keep the new one. Do not hoard, and avoid clutter at all costs!

Keep your desk or work surface uncluttered, especially if you work from home. Never let things pile up. At the end of the day, put everything away so that the following morning you encounter a clean desk. I normally work at a boardroom table. I do not want a desk with drawers. My assistant gives me the file I am working on and puts it away when I am finished with it.

The out-of-sight and out-of-mind rule applies to your office, as well as to everything in your home, including dirty dishes, the rubbish bin, and vacuuming. When an appliance breaks, get rid of it.

I give away clothes every six to nine months to make room for any new clothes I may have bought. I could purchase three additional wardrobes, but I don't because I don't believe in hoarding. I remember when my great aunt passed away. My mother spent months going through her cupboards, sorting and giving or throwing most things away. I vowed that, apart from my library of more than 3,000 books, I would not hoard clothes or anything else. I believe in travelling light in my journey of life.

Managing other people's expectations is critical to managing your life. Do not place unnecessary stress on yourself by promising delivery dates that aren't realistic and thereby letting people down. It is better to say that a task will take one or two days more than you expected and then surprise them by delivering early. Set yourself up for success, not failure.

With emails, people today expect virtually instant responses. If you aren't comfortable with that, let people know that you will respond within twenty-four hours. I check my emails once or twice a day. It is not my job to check my inbox constantly. I have an assistant who does that for me. I am surprised by how many people with a personal assistant continue to monitor their emails constantly, like an obsession.

Nothing drains our energy more than incompletion, whether it is money you owe or owed to you, books you borrowed that should be returned to their owners, or tasks and projects that need processing and completing. Create a system that works for you and prioritize it so that nothing gnaws at you and depletes your energy.

Only commit to doing those things that you are certain you can fulfil and no more, even if you are volunteering. Learn to say "no." We all need to be able to say "no" in order to avoid stress, resentment, and encroachment building up in our personal lives. As I like to say, "When in doubt, opt out."

We can choose to control our lives or let other people, our phones, or our emails control us. I decided to remove all email and other notifications from my smartphone. Now I only check my phone when I choose to.

To discern what is truly important, we must ask ourselves two simple but powerful questions:

- What is the best use of my time?
- How much is my time worth?

Place a monetary value on your time. Whether you decide to give it away for free or for a specific amount, you'll know exactly how much money you are giving away.

Carve out quiet time for reflection each day, ideally in the morning or evening, depending on your preference. It will help you discern and prioritize your activities. Personally, I like to rise early to connect with the most peaceful part of the day.

I also recommend taking a power nap in the afternoon. Ten to fifteen minutes is enough to rejuvenate. It is the secret weapon of many successful entrepreneurs.

My experience is that people who go to sleep when it gets dark and rise early with the sun, like the birds, will find their pot of gold—especially when they prepare for the day the night before.

DEPARTMENTALIZE YOUR LIFE

An effective way to manage your time that you can apply both at work and at home is to make a list of all your activities. Then, assign each activity a colour and select a day in your diary to devote exclusively to that type of activity. Whenever you see a blue day in your diary, for example, you will know exactly what to do that day. If for example you happen to work in sales, your most important activity will be to meet with clients. You could set aside blue days for meeting with clients the entire day and nothing else.

The next activity you designate may relate to paperwork and administration, arranging client meetings, or prospecting for new clients. Diarise those days in your calendar in another colour, perhaps yellow.

The final colour could be green for revitalization. Perhaps you will want to spend them on building relationships with a spouse, friends, and children, or by going on vacation. On a green day, you wouldn't read a magazine that relates to business or call the office. You would only use a green day to free up your mind and renew your energy.

Whatever you do in life, you can apply this highly effective system, to the extent applicable in your situation. Compartmentalising is a simple but powerful tool. When practiced regularly, you will experience each day as fresh. Nothing is carried over from the preceding day. Even more importantly, it removes stress by directing your daily activity, whether it's working on administration or meeting with a client. Your energy will move freely, and you will live each day with anticipation and excitement, with the spirit of "*Carpe diem!*"*

CONTEMPLATIONS: QUESTIONS TO ASK YOURSELF

Ask yourself the following questions and take the time to reflect on your answers.

1. How do you feel about asking others for help?

2. How flexible do you think you are in the various situations of your life?

The more flexible we are—which does not mean we allow ourselves to be pushed around—the more we control our environment, whether at work, at home, or within ourselves.

Be kind to yourself, appreciate yourself, and, most of all,

---
* Inspired by the work of Dan Sullivan.

love yourself. If you don't, you reject the hand that created you and will be unable to recognize the beauty of your being.

3. **To what extent do you take care of yourself emotionally and physically? What plan can you put in place to show yourself that you do?**

4. **If you had to flee your home in a fire, what would you risk your life to go back in and grab?** Whatever it is sheds light on what is most important to you and on what you should dedicate quality time to.

5. **Do you give yourself permission to enjoy life? If not, why?**

Enjoying life is a by-product of managing your time well. When you are free of stress and everything is in its place, you create space and clarity.

6. **What is your big "why?" What is the most important thing you want to pursue, create, or achieve that will put a fire in your belly?**

7. **What is your higher purpose?**

Find something you wish to do or be involved with that gets you up like a lion each morning, something that is bigger than yourself and includes other people or the planet.

8. Make a list of everything in your life that you would throw overboard if you were on a ship that was in danger of sinking. The list could include old clothes you no longer wear or commitments you no longer want—anything you don't want in your life.

If your list includes people, be sure to give reasonable notice where appropriate so that no one feels suddenly dumped. Always look after your reputation.

Be resolute in your decisions and don't allow anyone to talk you out of anything you decide to do or not do.

CHAPTER SEVEN

Abundance by Design

FINANCIAL AWARENESS AND THE IMPORTANCE OF CREATING RESOURCES

Retirement at sixty-five is ridiculous. When I was sixty-five, I still had pimples.
—GEORGE BURNS

To live a good life, you need resources.

Would you like to visit warm sandy beaches when you retire? Would you like to spend time with your grandchildren? Do you want to travel and discover new destinations? Do you want enough money to pay for care if you need it? Do you want to grow old with dignity and independence in the comfort of your own home, and not with strangers in an old people's home?

My father worked hard and provided well for my mother. She is cared for, in her old age, by two people round the clock. They look after her and keep her company, even though her family is never far away. We are fortunate that we all live in the same city.

When I worked in the financial services industry, I spoke to clients as young as twenty or thirty years of age about providing financially for their retirement. Sometimes I asked them if they knew that they would need to invest in retirement as much as half a million pounds ($700,000 USD) at 5 percent per annum interest in order to generate an annual income of £25,000 ($35,000 USD). Were they aware that money loses value and, assuming 5 percent inflation, half a million pounds would be worth only £306,000 ($428,000 USD) (nearly half the original amount) in ten years' time? In other words, did they know that the purchasing power of their income would nearly halve in ten years? Were they money savvy?

Would you be able to have a good life on half of your income if suddenly your salary was slashed? If it were to happen tomorrow, would it be a terrible blow to the quality of your life? What makes you think life would be fun if you didn't have adequate resources when you retire? The company you work for will take you out for a meal, shake your hand, and say goodbye. You will be much older than you are today and will feel more vulnerable.

When you are old, you will require the same resources that you need now. You may have your mortgage paid off and your children may be self-sufficient, but you will have at least eight more hours of free time a day, which will be fun only if you have the income to enjoy it.

KEEP YOUR FEET ON THE GROUND

Molly was one of my most powerful mentors. She was as wise as an owl and had a powerful presence and smiling blue eyes. If she had been in the epic *Star Wars* film, she would have been a Jedi Master. She used to say to me, "Always keep your feet firmly on the ground, Kenneth."

The best advice is the simplest. In fact, it may seem so simple that you risk not taking it seriously. For example, the present moment is the moment of potential—the moment in which everything is possible and in a state of becoming.

Imagine switching off your bedside lamp. The bulb goes out when the current of electricity is broken. The same is true in creation. If the current of universal energy were to stop, the universe would go into oblivion and disappear.

Therefore, every moment is injected with the energy that sustains all. Everything is created each moment. Because there is never an interruption in the flow of life, we are not aware of each new moment of creation and we take it for granted. Existence is always in a state of becoming. Everything is reinvented each second, including our potential to create.

Life happens in the present moment. Everything else is a memory of the past or an anticipation of the future. The problem is that we connect our emotions with fictional scenes that we run on the screen of our minds. We treat what we see there as if it were true. Sometimes, a thought about the future can make us freeze and be unable to function. Fear makes us procrastinate.

If you believe that you will not have financial security to enjoy the twilight years of your life, do something about it now rather than imagining the situation, worrying about it, or ignoring it as if it will never happen.

MAKING SMART CHOICES

Why do you think some of us create success in our lives and some of us don't? I believe it is because we filter our present experiences through our memories.

Our memories can be empowering or not. Let me illustrate my point with an example:

My friend and I are taking a vacation and leaving for Hawaii. We have been planning our trip for months. A year ago, I was travelling on a plane which had to crash land, and I thought I was going to die. My friend, on the other hand, has only had happy experiences of travel, especially on airplanes. He vividly remembers the excitement of going to Disney World with his parents and siblings. We are now sitting on the plane waiting to leave for Hawaii. Do you reckon we will each filter our experience of the journey differently? Of course, we will.

Here is another example:

Consider an imaginary character named Rick. When Rick was ten years old, the stock market crashed, and his father lost everything, including his job. The family house was repossessed, and the family went to live with their grandmother in a small, two-bedroom apartment on the other side of town where Rick had no friends. As if that wasn't enough, Rick's parents, who until then had a happy life together, started arguing about money. The atmosphere in the tiny apartment was unbearable.

What sort of relationship do you think Rick is going to have with money when he becomes an adult? Could his perception of money be different from someone who grew up not having to suffer the challenges Rick and his family faced? Could Rick end up filtering his life through a belief system that says money is the root of all evil, while his cousin, who is ten years younger and didn't experience the devastating effects of the stock market crash, doesn't?

We acquire freedom when we become aware of the source of our beliefs and how those beliefs mould our lives. What happened in your life and in the world around you when you were ten years old?

WHAT ABOUT DESTINY?

What in our destiny is not predetermined and cast in stone?

I believe there are destinies for people who don't make choices and destinies for people who do. Procrastination leads to a destiny of being stuck and unhappy, which then leads to boredom, depression, anger, cravings, over-indulgence, and even disease. Not making choices is like being in hell and not looking for the way out.

I have wanted to write this book for a while. Once I made the decision to do it and took appropriate action, the book became a reality, which is a form of magic if you think about it.

The action you take is your magic wand and you are the magician, like the universe saying your wish is its command. But first you must take credible and decisive action. You must prove that you are not wasting anyone's time, including yours. When you take one strategic step at a time, you begin to make progress.

My life experience has shown me that it is as simple as that. Set money aside in a box every day and within a year, or perhaps sooner, the box will be full of money. Squander money every day, and you will have nothing in a year's time.

We all have the power to engage with life and create whatever we want, but first we must take one step forward. If you don't start the car and put it into first gear, it will not move. We understand this when it comes to driving a car, but many of us don't understand this simple principle when it comes to steering our lives.

FOCUS ON WHAT YOU WANT

I know a person who complains that he is unlucky because life never gives him what he wants. In addition to generating negative energy by complaining, he is training his unconscious mind to deliver scarcity. He is not conscious of his good health and of having a wonderful family, which he should be grateful for.

I believe that in the same way a skyscraper needs sound foundations, we need to be grateful for what we have so it will become our foundation for building upward. When we focus on negativity and lack gratitude, we create a negative destiny. The unconscious mind listens to our words and actions and uses them as evidence for delivering more of the same. Remember what Deepak Chopra said, "Every cell in your body is eavesdropping on your internal dialogue." We become what we create.

YOU HAVE TO BE HUNGRY

If you have not eaten for a week, food will constantly be on your mind. You wouldn't be able to think about anything else. That is the nature of hunger.

When you want to create abundance in your life, you have to be hungry in the same way you are when your stomach is empty. You must think about abundance all day long, no matter what you are doing.

The reason people generate thirty thousand dollars per annum (and not per month) is not so much because they don't know how, but because they are not hungry enough. If they were hungry, they would find the way to earn more and not design their lives according to a lower level of income. They would stop saying that they can't afford what they want or that what they want is only for the rich.

I know a person who is unhappy in her job and feels it is not challenging. She said her life was stagnant. The problem she really had, however, was that her situation didn't hurt enough for her to take action and find the remedy.

I tried helping her by reframing the situation. I told her that it wasn't so much that her job wasn't challenging; rather, she wasn't challenging herself. Problems are never about what happens outside of us, I explained, but are about how we process those problems within ourselves.

The company the woman works for pays her a reasonable wage, and she in return gives them her time. The salary allows her to pay her bills and take an annual vacation. Instead of thinking of having a wage, I asked her to imagine her salary as a scholarship. In addition to the work she does during the day, she should do research for three or four hours in the evening as one would do if one was receiving a scholarship. For a few weeks or months, she would not be able to watch TV or go out every evening.

I told her to research two areas: 1) the latest business trends with a view to starting a business, and 2) the job market for well-paying, fulfilling jobs with great prospects.

Then I asked her to produce a two-part report. The first part was to be a short two-page business plan that identified market opportunities in her field. The second part was to focus on the jobs she found that fit her criteria.

If she acts as if she is receiving a scholarship and needs to fulfil the assignment, she will take massive action, move toward opportunity, and progress away from stagnation and boredom.

Are you hungry for abundance, prosperity, and fulfilment? Do you want to make your current annual income your monthly income while working half the number of hours you now do?

It can be done. I did it, but I was hungry—obsessively hungry for progress, as if I had not eaten for a week. Hunger is the magic wand. It takes you to the other side of the barrier that causes you to stagnate and prevents you from moving forward.

IT'S NOT ABOUT THE LOVE OF MONEY

Our economic system is underpinned by transactions and works relatively well most of the time. Whether we like it or not, without money we are unable to experience much of what is available in life. We can have anything we want, provided we pay for it.

A member of my business team recently jumped on a

plane with her husband and travelled to Hawaii to celebrate their wedding anniversary. Most people want to travel and discover the planet, and why shouldn't they?

Life is also a journey. We arrive here as a baby and, as we get older, we want to do as much as we can before packing our bags and leaving again. Life, wherever it comes from, is a gift and you don't question gifts. You embrace and enjoy them.

I find it fun when people sitting next to me on a plane open up and tell me their life story. I once sat next to someone who complained about not having enough money to do the things he loved. In the same breath, however, he claimed that money was not important to him, adding that he had a friend who was "swimming in it" and utterly unhappy in his life.

Money is important because it provides us with the ability to purchase what we need and want to have and experience. Money, of course, is not everything in life, but it certainly ranks up there with oxygen, unless you want to sit at home looking at four walls and worrying about how you are going to pay the next gas bill.

INDEPENDENCE AND FREEDOM

I believe it is important to invest time in developing one's financial literacy in order to progress. In life, you can either focus on dependence or independence. I have always wanted to shine my torch on independence. The more financially independent I am, the more freedom I have.

The handyman who comes to do odd jobs around our house has a great sense of humour. When he leaves, I say to him, "See you tomorrow, Jose." He always replies, "Not if I win the lottery tonight." I love that. It says everything. The only problem with his point is that a wealth mindset does not depend on winning the lottery. It depends on one's hunger for taking action now.

DEVELOPING A WEALTH MINDSET

In a mere thirteen years, I went from selling books door-to-door to growing and owning a multi-million-dollar financial services business with a client base of nine thousand. Some of my clients were international banks and multinational corporations. My market was a miniscule city of three square miles with a working population of eighteen thousand people. After thirteen years, I sold the company and began the first of my many retirements.

In truth, I will never retire, though I live as if I have. I don't have the patience to work at the same thing day in and day out for forty or fifty years. I love to learn and create, not merely maintain. For me, work is fun because I keep reinventing myself through new businesses and projects.

I have worked since I was thirteen years old. At the age of seventeen, I told my mum that I wanted to build a business like a poet writes poetry.

Whilst my friends played at the beach during the school summer holidays, I worked as a labourer in an industrial laundry, where the temperature reached 43 degrees Celsius (110 degrees Fahrenheit). I worked alongside adults and was paid the same wage as them.

Freedom has always been my motivation and is essential to my life. When I received an envelope with my paycheck at the end of the week, I felt independent.

My work ethic comes in part from my parents. I learned from them that if I didn't have enough money to buy or do what I wanted, I could not rely on anyone else to get it for me. Growing up, I never asked my family for money. When as a young man I wanted to go to university in the United Kingdom, I was turned down when I applied for a government grant and my father couldn't afford to pay my expenses. Fortunately, I had saved enough money to pay for everything myself and graduate debt-free.

I moved to London when I was twenty in order to gain

some life experience. I saw an advert in the newspaper for a job pressing suits at a factory. Because I had worked in a laundry in Gibraltar, I thought I would be able to do the work. I hadn't done any pressing at the laundry, but I had seen adults use the machines.

I phoned the factory, told them I had experience and was told to come by at six the next morning.

When I arrived, I saw rows and rows of suits waiting to be pressed. Pressers were expertly turning them out, one a minute. I was able to press one suit in an hour. Three hours after I started at the factory, I was fired. But I never felt it was a negative experience. On the contrary, trying to press suits reconfirmed my work ethic and my willingness to take risks. I was paid for my three hours of work, and I patted myself on the back for making some money. I hadn't wasted my time. I had learned, made a few pounds (dollars), and had a story to tell. Potential failure has never held me back. Perhaps failing the exam at age eleven instilled in me a fighting spirit, a rallying cry, which has served me well throughout my life. Moreover, my suit pressing story has been hugely profitable as I have shared it with audiences all over the world.

One of the foundation stones of a wealth mindset is perseverance. Shortly after the suit pressing experience, I was given an opportunity to work in the administration department of a menswear wholesaler, which in turn led to a job as the manager of a famous menswear store in King's Road, Chelsea. The store was part of an upmarket, luxury chain and was popular among movie stars and pop musicians. The actress Virginia McKenna, who starred in the film *Born Free*, frequently stopped by to shop for her son.

The managerial job required perseverance because I had no previous experience in the field. When the question about whether I had managed a shop of similar size came up in the interview, as I knew it would, I crossed my fingers behind my back, asked my Creator for forgiveness and replied, "Yes, of course. I managed the leading menswear store in Gibraltar for two years."

I was hungry! I wanted a break, and I knew I could deliver. When I left the job to return to Gibraltar three years later, the managing director wrote me a brilliant reference and said that there would always be a job for me if I ever wanted to return.

During my first few days on the job, I stayed at the store until well past midnight to acquaint myself with the chain's administrative systems and other details. I was in charge of people twice my age, though I had never before managed people. After two years, the store went from thirty-fifth in the chain, in terms of performance and productivity, to number three. We could easily have been number one, I believe, if the shop had been larger. Our store was one-third the size of two others located in central London. I succeeded in managing the store because I was hungry and was prepared to do whatever it took.

That was many years ago, and I have since built important businesses, but I still refer to the experience with much affection. It was my first significant job in a major city as a young person, and it taught me that people who are hungry succeed in life. I continue to be as hungry today as I was back then. I am always searching, creating, learning, and grateful for the wonderful adventure of life.

WHERE IS YOUR MIND TAKING YOU?

Today, many young people graduate from university and take a long time to look for a job. They insist on finding a job that is related to their area of study. A wealth mindset, in contrast, is about taking responsibility and being independent, irrespective of whether a job is related to one's academic studies or not.

By the time I was twenty, I knew working for an employer as a store manager wasn't going to make me wealthy, but my mindset was, "*Take action, and do an honest day's work.*" That and other jobs eventually led to my starting my own business and being able to create real wealth.

Wealth is not related solely to the amount of money we have in the bank. It includes our state of mind and having a positive attitude toward growing, developing, and preparing ourselves for the next job or business opportunity.

EVERYTHING IS FOR THE GOOD

With a wealth mindset, you understand that all your experience is for the ultimate good of everything you come in contact with. If you don't get the job you want or your businesses fails, instead of being disappointed, you remain confident, consider how much you learned, have faith, and search for something even better. You always do your best and detach from the outcome. The outcome is outside of your control.

BE CREATIVE, NOT COMPETITIVE

Creativity, not competitiveness, fuels wealth acquisition.

When I started my financial services firm, there was a great deal of competition in the marketplace. Some companies had been in the business for many years.

After I qualified for membership in the Million Dollar Roundtable, the premier international trade association for insurance brokers and financial advisors, I travelled every year to the United States to attend the annual meeting. Those on my sales team who qualified to attend would join me. We learned about the latest ideas and innovations in our field. After returning home, we implemented many of the techniques we had been introduced to in our small town. My competitors used to say that travelling to the other side of the world to attend the meeting was a waste of time and money.

We also adopted another key concept of the wealth mindset—the recognition that success is based on the value you bring to the market. The Million Dollar Round Table taught me that when you deliver value, not only do you acquire a client, you also create a friendship. Consequently, we positioned ourselves in the marketplace in a unique way.

Over the years, I received feedback from people who told me that I had created a positive revolution in the insurance industry in Gibraltar. Sir Peter Caruana, the chief minister of Gibraltar at the time, said at the inauguration of our new offices in the Natwest Building that I had brought marketing to Gibraltar that had never been used there before.

Apart from sound professionalism, honesty, and a strong work ethic, we had love and enthusiasm for our clients, the industry, and the marketplace. We felt a sense of gratitude for our success, which made us feel responsible for the value we delivered. We were hungry not only to succeed, but to succeed well and with pride and care. We planted a beautiful garden that would survive the test of time.

Once the managing director of one of our competitors said to me at a Chamber of Commerce dinner that he never understood what it was that made our company successful. Many of our original competitors are no longer in business; however, the company I founded on a rock solid foundation years ago continues to deliver value and is a household name in Gibraltar.

PURPOSE AND WEALTH

Possessing purpose is a characteristic of a wealth mindset. Part of my purpose is to support my family and create a protective shield around them so that they can maximize the opportunities in their lives. With that in mind, I made my father chairman of my company in recognition of how hard he had worked during his life and for the massive value he brought to my business.

I also consider creating employment for others, paying taxes to contribute to the well-being of my country, and offering products and services that help people better their lives to be part of my purpose. I believe a wealth mindset can embrace the desire to help others whilst also honouring and respecting oneself.

Many years after starting my company, a member of my sales team who had been with me from the beginning said to me that looking back on her experience building the business, she felt it had been similar to a spiritual experience. She acknowledged the impact we had on helping others whilst, at the same time, serving our own desire to prosper and thrive.

We built a business from seemingly nothing, but that is not really true. The desire to create, with a love for the purpose, is what produced something from nothing. It was like turning metal into gold or transforming a blank canvas into a work of art.

STEADY AS SHE GOES

In order to possess a wealth mindset, you have to build self-esteem. We build self-esteem by keeping our commitments and finishing the tasks we embark on.

We succeed by being both hungry and patient—hungry for success and willing to take three steps forward and one step back, if necessary, to reposition ourselves. As I fly my life forward, I tell myself, "Steady as she goes, Kenneth. Aim for the star at the end of the galaxy."

Never settle for small. Be ambitious. Have your cake and eat it too! Who says you can't when you are being creative?

On our life journey, it is critical to regularly acknowledge what we have achieved. Make recognition of your accomplishments the fuel that powers you forward.

ARE YOU UNEMPLOYABLE?

Not long ago, I was asked to speak at a conference held at Regent's University, London. Some years prior, I had completed a master's degree at this wonderful university located in Regent's Park.

I was invited to address a theatre filled with academics and university personnel from approximately twenty universities located around the world. When I finished speaking, I was asked to elaborate on what it takes to be an entrepreneur. I believe the person who asked for additional information was involved in designing entrepreneurship courses and wanted to fully understand what I had said.

I thought for a moment and replied, "An entrepreneur is unemployable." I don't think anyone in the room expected that reply.

I continued, "You see, what motivates me as an entrepreneur is freedom—to live in my dream and not in someone else's dream, to create something successful from nothing, and to have the sky as my limit."

I did not mean to say that an entrepreneur could not perform well as an employee. I meant that if freedom is as important as oxygen; by its very nature it makes you unemployable.

THE PATH TO WEALTH

The quickest path to wealth is starting and scaling one's own business. Nothing in life is guaranteed, of course, and everything carries a risk, but I prefer to take risks that I can manage rather than be in a situation in which another person manages the risk.

Recently, one of the biggest airlines in the UK failed overnight, leaving thousands of long-standing, loyal employees unemployed. Many of those employees were interviewed in the evening news and seemed incredulous. Suddenly, they didn't have a job. What was going to happen to them? It makes you think whether you are more secure working for someone else or having your own business.

LEARN HOW TO SELL

In sales, you strive to develop an investigative style that tactfully searches for the client's needs so that you give the client what he or she wants. Most of the time, what the client wants is concealed, and you have to help them uncover it.

No one ever came to see me with the desire to buy life insurance during my years in the financial services industry. I had to help my clients discover how much they loved their families and how, above all else if they were to die prematurely, they wanted their families to continue living the life they had created for them.

I once went to see the partners of one of the leading law firms in my city. They implied I was wasting my time as they were not interested in buying life insurance. I took a flip chart with me and had written the names of their children and spouses on the front sheet. As they looked up, they were surprised to see the names of their families. I told them that in the same way they represented people in court that I was there representing their families so that they wouldn't suffer any financial hardship in the event that they died prematurely. Within minutes, they all agreed to buy considerable amounts of life insurance. I just gave them the opportunity to discover how much they loved their families.

A client will buy from you instead of you having to sell to a client if what is uppermost in your mind is the client's well-being. That is how my company acquired nine thousand clients in a city with a working population of eighteen thousand. We cared and sought to build long-term relationships.

I discussed the importance of legacy in a previous chapter,

and the point I want to make now is similar. When you build a trusting relationship with a client, your business will become part of their legacy when they introduce you to their next generation.

BECOMING A BUSINESS OWNER

A successful business owner builds a management team that can run the business and not depend on the owner for progress. You have created yourself a job if the business needs you to be there 24/7 in order to survive.

A strong team is an important part of the purchase of a business. The person who bought my business was already in profit the moment we completed the deal. I consciously built the business from scratch, brick by brick and employee by employee, so that thirteen years later someone would pay a substantial amount of money for it. An investor will pay multiple times the annual profit of a business.

Today, one can build an internet business based on selling physical or digital products and make money while you sleep. The shopping cart is open twenty-four hours a day.

UNDERSTANDING ASSETS AND LIABILITIES

Many people fail to understand the difference between an

asset and a liability. An asset puts money in your pocket and a liability takes money out. Often people think their home is an asset, but if you are paying a mortgage to the bank and living in the property, you are not generating an income. The property is not an asset. It is a liability. A property only becomes an asset when it is sold or rented and puts money in your pocket.

Building and maintaining wealth requires being focused on and paying attention to when you are creating liabilities, committing to recurring expenses, and living beyond your means.

PAY YOURSELF FIRST

Decide what portion of your income you want to save each month and put it aside before you pay anyone. Generate an income which supports that plan. Your life will depend on it.

Aim, dream, research, and aspire to make your annual income your monthly income. Do not settle for less. Plodding along is not good for your physical or financial health.

Imagine earning twelve times what you currently earn and spending three to four hours each evening away from the TV doing research necessary to achieve it.

Be present every moment of the day. What is going on

around you? What are people saying? What are people buying? How can you do something better than the way it is being done now? What unique value do you bring to the market? What are your unique abilities that people comment on? How can you monetize those abilities?

Create wealth by building a business. Start on a part-time basis until the income from the business can replace your current salary. Then you are free.

My goal has always been to save no less than 50 percent of what I earn. That means I have to be massively creative, enthusiastic, happy, and in love with my life. You have to be willing to earn more than you need for today in order to fund the life that you want tomorrow.

Break through the glass ceiling because, in truth, whatever might be holding you back are invented perceptions! Claim your freedom.

In the words of Jessie B. Rittenhouse:

> *I bargained with Life for a penny,*
> *And Life would pay no more,*
> *However I begged at evening*
> *When I counted my scanty store.*
> *For Life is a just employer,*
> *He gives you what you ask,*

But once you have set the wages,
Why, you must bear the task.
I worked for a menial's hire,
Only to learn, dismayed,
That any wage I had asked of Life,
Life would have willingly paid.

CONTEMPLATIONS: QUESTIONS TO ASK YOURSELF

The following questions and contemplations will help you determine whether you are creating sufficient resources to live a good life:

1. Do I have enough money to last the rest of my life? If not, what I am going to do about it, beginning today?

2. Am I unconsciously neglecting my health and, thereby, planning my demise because I won't have enough money to support myself for the rest of my life? If that is the case, what am I going to do to resolve the situation?

3. Imagine you travel into the future and you meet the elderly person you will one day become. What will they say to you if you haven't provided for them properly?

"You abandoned me. You had the opportunity to provide for me in my old age, and you didn't. I can't afford a car which I desperately need or a vacation in the sun to warm my old, aching bones. Did you think that because I am old I wouldn't need the same things you need as a young person? Things still break and need to be replaced. I would love to visit my grandchildren. I miss them, am lonely, and cannot afford the trip. Soon I am going to need care, and I don't have money to provide for myself. What is going to become of me? Am I going to end up a number in an old person's home, sharing a room with a stranger? Are they going to treat me kindly and with love? Who is going to be with me when I die? Please, go back. Go back and consider starting a business. Do anything, but don't let this happen to you when you get here."

4. If you don't now enjoy financial independence, why do you think that is?

- What is it that you are prepared to do to create financial independence in your life?
- Make a list of what you are going to need to do in order to create financial independence in your life.
- How will you be able to confirm that you have reached your goal of having financial independence?
- What will financial independence do for you and permit you to do?
- Are you prepared to take massive action and full responsibility for achieving financial independence?
- When you arrive at your goal, what will your life look

like with regard to people, places, timelines, and your ability to plan for a positive and motivating future?
- Please refer now to the full visualization exercise before the contemplations at the end of chapter 3 and create an image of yourself in a life of abundance and financial independence.
- I knew financial independence could be achieved as I have seen other people work to become financially independent. Do you know anybody who has? Guess what; you know me, and if I could do it so can you.
- So, let's summarize and find your purpose for enjoying a life of abundance and financial independence. Please answer these questions:
    - Why do you want to be financially independent?
    - What will take place in your life when you are financially independent?
    - What will not manifest in your life when you are financially independent?
    - If you don't build your resources and become financially independent, what will be missing in your life?*

5. Do I sleep well, free of resentments from the past?

There is an imaginary bridge which connects today with tomorrow. We must all sleep well at night in order to cross over that bridge and feel refreshed in the morning. Many

---
* Inspired by the work of Tad James.

of us carry emotional baggage across the bridge each night and continue to carry it around with us wherever we go. It is heavy and debilitating. Perhaps you may need help from a qualified life coach or psychologist to get rid of your baggage. At some point, we all need help in our lives. If that is your situation, take action today. Get help and work on getting rid of toxic luggage.

6. Write a letter to your parents, even if they have passed away. Tell them everything that is in your heart.

I wrote a text for my parents (see sidebar) one night, and it helped me appreciate them more than I had ever done before. Primarily, it helped me understand that they were human beings who did their best from their level of awareness. We often hold our parents accountable as if they were gods. Doing this exercise with inspirational music in the background set me free.

It will also help you if you have the courage to have a peaceful yet powerful conversation with your parents or anyone else for whom you may be harbouring resentment or ill feelings. People die, and it is unfair to them and you to not clear resentments before it is too late. Life is challenging enough without having to carry a heavy load on your back.

Take the initiative. Don't wait for others to come to you.

Go to them. Making peace will free up your energy, and doors will suddenly open in your life that were previously shut and you didn't know why.

HONOUR MY PARENTS

It was five in the morning, and I got up to work on my new book. Instead, my soul decided we were going on a journey.

I wrote on a piece of paper: honour my parents.

My eyes welled up with tears. I was in my heart, swimming in an ocean of love. I was inside my parents' love for me—a one-way lane of unconditional love, which until that moment I had never experienced.

A magical place had opened its doors to me and with soft eyes invited me to sit down in the middle of its existence. I was alone with myself in a place of love and knowing.

If it wasn't for my mother and my father, I wouldn't be here. They brought me into life, but much more than that. Everything that I am or ever hope to be I owe to my parents. None of my achievements would have been possible without them. They brought me into the world with unbounding love and an excitement which defies human logic.

As I journeyed powerfully through my life, I had been oblivious to the limited tools they had as human beings to cherish and nourish me, always as best they could. Their blessings and prayers became my protective shield in this amazingly mysterious, inside-out universe that we all journey in.

When things were hard, as they sometimes were, they fed and clothed me before attending to themselves and their needs. They made me feel wealthy, even though we were far from it. Who else in God's universe would have done that for me but my parents?

If someone else had, I would have climbed the highest peaks and proclaimed their kindness and love. Maybe a book would have been written in their honour and a television programme made about them.

Yet, my parents expected nothing in return. It was innate in them to give and never stop giving, with a kiss, a good word of encouragement, or a tender smile, even when they didn't feel like smiling.

It was not until I had children of my own and they became adults that this magical place of realisation opened its doors to me, which I entered and then was set free.

CONCLUSION

Let Your Light Shine Bright

YOU ARE THE ONE!

As I end this book, I feel like many of us do when we send our children off into the world. We prepare them as best we can with our wisdom, experience, and advice as the day of their departure approaches. When the time comes to say goodbye, we want to squeeze in one last tip because of our desire to keep our children safe and protected as they venture forth into life. That is how I feel about you, dear reader, as I arrive at this conclusion. I have endeavoured at every step to reach out to you and give you my best, and I hope that in some humble way I have been able to contribute to your wonderful and magnificent life.

The benefits of making the changes for pursuing a healthy

body and mind that I suggest in this book are fundamental to having a happy life, making good decisions, and staying grounded.

YOU ARE THE BEST

You are the best, whether you believe it or not. In fact, you have no choice in the matter because you were created that way, despite what anyone may have said to you when you were growing up. We come into the world believing everything we are told. Even our name infuses our identity.

From a young age, people whom we perceived as an authority in our lives, such as parents, teachers, or older siblings, influenced who we believe we are. If someone said we were beautiful, sensitive, and smart, it is likely that we perceive ourselves as beautiful, sensitive, and smart. If we heard that we were clumsy, ugly and stupid, it could have influenced our personality growing up and how we engaged with life. We let our light shine brighter or dimmer in accordance with what we believe is true about ourselves.

The beliefs we hold about ourselves are not all negative. Many of them can be empowering, but all of them are invented, and we live our life unconsciously proving them to be true every step of the way.

Imagine there is a child inside of you—a cute, lovable child whom you want to kiss, hug, care for, and protect. That child is who you are. It has always been there, and it is as innocent and powerful as it was the day you were born.

Now imagine holding the child in your arms. What advice would you give the child if you wanted it to have the best life possible? What would you want it to believe as it develops and grows?

TAKE ACTION NOW

There comes a time in life to take a courageous step forward and break free of the negative agreements and narratives that shackle and limit you and your possibilities. Disentangle yourself from hidden resentments of the past and any fears you may have about an imagined future.

As I've mentioned, we carry our baggage across a bridge each night while sleeping and wake with it in the morning. None of the baggage is true and it has no value. It exists only in our thoughts.

Tonight, throw your baggage into the sea before crossing the bridge. All that matters is the here and now—the only place where you can take massive action. Keep only those agreements that empower you. Life presents us with enough challenges without you fighting a battle from within yourself. Freedom is your heritage.

Whether you feel ready or not, take massive action now. In your mind, see yourself standing in front of a sword embedded in a stone. Place your hands around the handle of the sword and pull it out effortlessly. Become aware of the power within you and of who you were born to be. You were created to be powerful. Now is the time to stop trying to prove otherwise. When we resist expressing our personal power, we create the foundation for a life riddled with problems.

Take the sword with you, mount the beautiful horse that awaits you and ride through the streets of your kingdom. Notice the many people, some of whom you recognize, who have come out to cheer you on and celebrate with you. When you liberate yourself, you give others permission to do the same. You cannot imagine the number of people you influence without realising it.

I will always cheer you on. Even as I write this conclusion, I am cheering you and celebrating with you.

Your mission now, if you choose to accept it, is to encourage others to bring light and love—the only truth there is—into the world. Light and love connect us all and doesn't exclude anyone. You see it in the eyes of a baby. We must work to let light and love shine through us every day.

Wake up from the deep slumber of invented notions that

we all have slept in for too long, and softly and lovingly begin to awaken your brothers and sisters who journey with us. Our lineage is royalty, and our inheritance is founded on the legacy we leave behind.

Some people who are still asleep might laugh and be sceptical, but don't let your love be diminished. When the time is right, they will wake up, too.

Remember to stay in the here and now and to focus on what you want, not on what you don't want. Your journey can be compared to travelling on a train and stopping at many stations along the way. At some stations, we experience happiness, inspiration, joy, fulfilment, and empowerment. At other stations, we may experience sadness, uncertainty, overwhelm, frustration, boredom, despair, and depression.

Learn a lesson at each station, but don't lose sight of the journey. Get back on the train and leave the station forever once you have learned the lesson. There is no need to return to the same station ever again. The lessons you learn at each station belong to you and become part of your experience and your wisdom. The universe loves you too much to give you charity, so the gift is the lesson you work hard to learn. We must take full responsibility for the results, because, consciously or not, we are the ones who designed the journey and chose the stations where our train will stop in order to learn the lessons we seek.

When we live this way, we continue to seek opportunities. We move forward on our hero's journey. Our self-esteem rises each time we complete a project and master a situation.

You will no longer react to life, but will respond instead. You will watch your thoughts and find the space between them so that you get out of your head and become fully present.

Life does not go around and around in a monotonous way. It moves in an upward spiral, enabling us to carry with us the wisdom we have acquired.

In Chapter 4, I told you the story of the prisoner who was given the choice of a firing squad or going through a door to the unknown. The prisoner chose the firing squad because he feared the unknown, and he died. It was later revealed that on the other side of the door there was nothing except his freedom, but he was too frightened to choose it.

Are you ready to walk boldly through the door into the unknown and claim your purpose, freedom, and abundance? Are you willing to tap into your magnificence and be who you were born to be? Honour yourself. The choice is yours to make.

May you always find the courage to be the blessing in your life.

God speed to you, my dear friend. I love you.

EPILOGUE

A New World

She was a princess, living in a kingdom of lies—a land deeply subservient to a book of rules which made up the dream of the kingdom. A fiction which held the minds of its victims in captivity.

The cruel wizard who ruled the kingdom controlled the lives of the people by putting them under a spell. He made them believe that they were less rather than more and that they should judge themselves harshly whenever they did not comply with the book of rules.

When a baby was born and as soon as it took its first breath, a new cycle of domestication began. Loving parents, well-meaning teachers, older siblings, and the culture of the place in which the baby lived were surreptitiously used by the wizard to program the child's mind. This process continued until the person became old and took their last breath.

The people journeyed blindly like cattle in a field, unconsciously yearning to fill a gaping void. One day, the princess and her brothers and sisters began to wake up in the here and now from the deep hypnotic slumber which had held them down. As they did so, they discovered their magnificence through the vast cosmos within them. The wizard lost his power and disappeared into oblivion, never to be seen again.

They could now see that all the limiting beliefs that had been instilled into their minds had been lies and that they had unconsciously played small* out of fear of stepping out of their comfort zone and seeking opportunity. They became aware that they were of royal descent.

They realised that the wizard had driven a wedge between them, which had led them to live as enemies in the bowels of hell for millennia.

The princess and her brothers and sisters saw that they were all one and rejoiced and lived in peace, harmony, and freedom all the days of their lives.

---

* Dequiana Jackson, "5 Ways Playing Small is Sabotaging Your Business," *Huffington Post*, March 31, 2016, https://www.huffingtonpost.com/entry/5-ways-playing-small-is-s_b_9579516.html.

Acknowledgments

My team of professionals, including my publisher, Kathleen Pedersen and my editors, Carol Raphael, Robyn Burwell, and Barbara Boyd who guided me with honesty, commitment, and professionalism.

My mentors throughout the years, Molly Ledwidge, Kit Sutton, Cyril Lesser, Norman G. Levine, and The Million Dollar Round Table.

Some of my teachers whose work has inspired my own: Deepak Chopra, Tad James, Helen Urwin, A.M. Krasner, Dan Sullivan, Carol S. Pearson, Don Miguel Ruiz, Thich Nhat Hanh and Robert Kiyosaki.

My wife, Maxine, for supporting me at every step, sustaining me with her delicious healthy food, encouraging me to write this book, investing many hours of her time reading my work and giving me invaluable feedback, and for contributing to the design of the book cover.

My children, Ben, Daniella, and Sarah, for the wisdom they bring into my life, for their highly professional and technical support as well as their unbounding love, freshness, enthusiasm, and commitment to my success.

My mother, Iris, for believing in me, encouraging me to always break the shackles, embrace freedom, and go for gold, and for being the most inspirational person I know who leads by example.

My late father Elias, a man of integrity, who taught me to be a critical thinker, to look before I leap, and gave me the inspiration that led me to change my lifestyle, embrace health and fitness, and write this book.

Gibraltar, the beautiful city I was born in and its wonderful and magnificent people.

My Creator for always daring me to win at the game of life.

About the Author

KENNETH CASTIEL is a British entrepreneur and angel investor, an inspiring speaker, success counsellor, and business philosopher. His first business venture was selling books door-to-door.

He later founded and went on to build the leading homegrown financial services corporation in Gibraltar, acquiring nine thousand clients out of a working population of eighteen thousand people.

He brought his industry together so that it could speak with one voice and was commended by the Financial Services Commissioner for doing so. He was also praised by the Chief Minister of Gibraltar for his integrity and for his marketing acumen "not seen in Gibraltar before."

He developed a powerful and highly motivated sales team who all qualified for the Million Dollar Round Table, the premiere association of financial professionals representing the top 5 percent of the industry worldwide.

Kenneth set up his financial services business from humble beginnings with a huge vision, a solid nonnegotiable commitment to succeed, and an exit strategy. Thirteen years later, he sold his multi-million-dollar corporation as the market leader in his industry.

Everything is always in a state of becoming, and so he went on to teach entrepreneurs how to replicate his success methods. His methodology shows people his legacy formula and the key to a life of purpose, freedom, and abundance.

He has embarked on cutting-edge education at the highest level in the fields of NLP and archetypal branding and returned to university to graduate through the school of psychotherapy and psychology at Regent's University, London with a master's degree in creative leadership.

His favourite hobby is going on extreme adventures with his entrepreneurial friends. He is the eighty-first civilian in the world to have done a military-style skydive out of an airplane at 30,000 feet, the cruising altitude of a commercial jet, and enjoyed cliff jumping into icy waters in Iceland. He also tobogganed down a glacier in Iceland using nothing but his own body. He is an avid reader, enjoys keeping fit, and loves life, people, and freedom.

Kenneth is married to Maxine, whom he met on an airplane 30,000 feet above the skies of Israel. They have three children.

Connect with Kenneth at:

https://www.kennethcastiel.com
https://www.facebook.com/kennethcastiel
https://www.instagram.com/kennethcastiel
https://www.twitter.com/kennethcastiel
https://www.linkedin.com

www.ingramcontent.com/pod-product-compliance
Lightning Source LLC
Chambersburg PA
CBHW032106090426
42743CB00007B/253